POETRY WRITING

THE EXPERT GUIDE

POETRY WRITING

THE EXPERT GUIDE

Fiona Sampson

ROBERT HALE · LONDON

© *Fiona Sampson 2009*
First published in Great Britain 2009

ISBN 978-0-7090-8541-6

Robert Hale Limited
Clerkenwell House
Clerkenwell Green
London EC1R 0HT

www.halebooks.com

A catalogue record for this book is available from the British Library

6 8 10 9 7 5

Typeset by
Derek Doyle & Associates, Shaw Heath
Printed in Great Britain by the MPG Books Group,
Bodmin and King's Lynn

Contents

For AAS and PMS,
keeping up the tradition.

1 What is poetry, anyway?

Who is Silvia? What is she,
That all our swains commend her?
William Shakespeare, *Two Gentlemen of Verona*

On the table in my shed I have a single piece of slate. Grit has worn notches, and in one place a small hole, in it. Whenever I get stuck I pick up this slate, which is about the size of my palm, and weigh it in my hand. Though my house is full of pebbles and shells, literal touchstones of places I've visited, it so happens that I didn't collect this piece. But it comes from a spot which, for me, symbolizes poetry. One September afternoon a couple of years ago, my Hungarian friend Peter went skinny-dipping in the bay between Dante's Rock and the castle at Duino, where Rainer Maria Rilke wrote his *Elegies*, and picked up this stone from the seabed. The castle overlooks the Adriatic. You can hear the sea at every window. Rilke's *Duino Elegies* are full of movement and beauty, too, but there's nothing picturesque or obvious about their flow of thought and image. They're doing something much more ambitious than simply describing scenery, however striking.

For the *Elegies* are a series of attempts at nothing less than transcendence, and what they try to transcend is, as their title suggests, death itself. These are pretty high stakes! Most poetry comes nowhere near even attempting them. But think about this for a moment, and perhaps it doesn't seem so crazy. After all, to make something – whether it's a poem, a family, a garden or a prototype rocket – is always to go beyond the limits of what you are. It's to make something exist *out there*, beyond the self. That's transcendence, in a way. If this is your perspective, it becomes a lot easier to take poetry seriously, to make it fit into your life and to want to do it well.

The souvenir on my table reminds me how high the stakes for poetry can be – and that's why I value it. But touchstones are personal: they're whatever poetry means to *you*. Many poets have pictures of writers by their desks. In Dylan Thomas's work-shed at Laugharne, fading newspaper and postcard images of Lord Byron, Walt Whitman, Louis MacNeice, W.H. Auden and William Blake are pinned to the wooden wall. The *Guardian* used to run a series on writers' rooms in its weekly 'Review' section. Along with family mementos and encouraging souvenirs of success, it seems many keep reminders of their writing heroes close to them as they work. For example, Andrew Motion owns the very copy of the *Oxford English Dictionary* that belonged to Philip Larkin, his early mentor and role model. He talks about the pleasure of consulting, every day, a reference tool Larkin must have handled in the very same way. Such touchstones aren't much different from the family photos and souvenirs in our living rooms. They help us remember where we want to belong and the kind of people we think we are.

So it's not surprising that we surround ourselves with them when we approach the magical and risky business of writing. Yet not all reminders are so tangible. There are touchstone *moments*, too. Think back to the first time you read a particular poem or poet, and your sense of what poetry could be changed. Or remember the teacher who gave you the sense that you were 'good at writing'. These guiding encounters are touchstones, and lodestones too – indeed, maybe there's no difference. For a touchstone is a compass with which to navigate the complex, often confusing, world of poetry. You can hold on to what matters to you without being afraid of finding out what you'll discover next.

Here are some examples. One touchstone for me was hearing Ted Hughes read at Hay-on-Wye, in the last year of his life. In those days, the literature festival was held in a big marquee by the river. As Hughes came to the microphone, a storm blew up out of a fine June day. The whole time he read the wind blew, canvas flapped, and rigging creaked. The moment he'd finished, the storm died down. Whatever caused that coincidence of the elements – Hughes was reading from *Birthday Letters*, a memoir of his famously stormy relationship with his wife Sylvia Plath – the experience was uncanny and undeniable. Another moment, much earlier but equally formative in its way, came when I was a child of five or six. My primary school headmaster read us the beginning of Dylan Thomas's *Under Milk Wood* in school assembly. Mr Griffiths also had a big presence and a fine reading voice. I understood very little of Thomas, except that I was experiencing something new. But I was bowled over.

These events put me in harm's way, as far as poetry went. And I've memories of other 'encounters' too: reading Edward Thomas's poem about the approach of death, 'Lights Out', in hospice; or the familiar beauty of liturgy in the church to which I was taken as a child. Re-living these memories always feels like stepping into a room where all the lights are on. Everything seems to be extra clear and to make so much sense. Since they actually happened, memories can't be negotiated away, as if they were just a sort of lucid dream. It's this fixed quality, of something that can be held in mind, that turns memories into touchstones. And poems seem to work in the same way. A good poem is a *vade-mecum*, something you can take with you wherever you go. It's the memorized lines the famous hostage recited over and over in the face of the unknown; it's a quotation like a proverb that sticks in your mind, a small certainty – certainty about its own terms at least – to hold on to when you're faced with something difficult, whether at work or in a relationship.

That certainty has a key role to play in poetry. The

American poet-doctor William Carlos William wrote that 'A poem is a small (or large) machine made of words'. The contemporary British poet Don Paterson has called a poem 'A small machine for remembering itself'. What both mean, I think, is that a well-made poem is a completed object, a whole to which every part contributes. It's also a completely achieved insight, moment or thought.

This wholeness of a poem is a little like three-dimensionality. You should be able to, as it were, walk round and view the poem from behind. When you take a close look at how it's constructed, maybe in the course of translating it into another language, or even in critical analysis, you should find it remains in one piece. It shouldn't lose resonance, or such formal qualities as balance. Nor should it turn out to be just a matter of style, or something that is full of poetic ideas but isn't yet a poem. However it's read, whether sloppily or with terrific care, a true poem should carry on being exactly itself.

So poems are like touchstones, and we approach the making of them by way of touchstones too. There's a continuous sequence running from the very first poem that interested you – perhaps in childhood – to the one you'll write today. Poems are objects, or moments, in a sequence of similar objects. That sequence is always opening up ahead of us, as both poets and readers, and is different for everyone. The Fibonacci number sequence makes its pattern entirely according to a logic that can't be imitated by any other approach – and nor can your own way into poetry.

So it's important to hold on to your personal sense of what poetry is. Poetry touchstones are like loves: there's no point in listing who you think they *ought* to be. If Marianne Moore doesn't do it for you, you can admire her work but there's no point trying to model yourself on it. What moves you about, and into, poetry is important *because* it's already done just that.

There are several ways to assemble your personal poetry touchstones. Use secondhand bookshops, on Amazon and in the non-virtual world, to locate the exact editions of books that changed your view of poetry for ever. Keep them on your desk. Stick postcard portraits of poets you admire by your computer. Deepen your knowledge of your touchstone poets by reading more widely in their work, or try the critical literature that surrounds them. Contemplate a poetry screen-saver: not necessarily a poem, but maybe a photo of a place that matters to the poetry reader in you. It could just be a snap from the holiday on which you first read, say, Derek Walcott. Or it could be the landscape associated with a poet: Nerja, setting for the tragic original of Federico Lorca's *Blood Wedding*; or R.S. Thomas's Lleyn peninsula.

There are things to do outside the home, too. If you can, take a weekend trip to any birthplace, museum or other site associated with one of your heroes. Join the Poetry Library, or the Scottish Poetry Library, even if you live so far out of town that you'll rarely be able to borrow books. Investigate any vestigial poetry section in your local library, and make a point of ordering at least two poetry collections you really value – just so that they have them in stock. Check out what, if any, poetry is available in your nearest bookshop. Resolve to order at least one book from there next time you want to buy, so staff get the idea that poetry might have the occasional customer.

Finally, make yourself sit down and list all those key moments that developed your interest in poetry. It doesn't matter whether you summarize what you remember on a scrap of paper the size of a business card and keep it in your wallet, or stick a decorative list on the fridge door, or type up an orderly account to keep in your computer. What's impor-tant is that you end up with a copy that you can use as a mnemonic whenever you're feeling a bit discouraged.

'Where do I come from?' is one of the most powerful ques-tions a child can ask. Remembering where you come from as a poet is powerful because it re-inspires and re-directs you, reminding you where you want and ought to be. It's a bit like a moral compass for your practice. Unless he's true to what he believes in, no writer will be more than a fake. One of the

11

secrets of genre writing is, famously, to enjoy that genre. That's even more the case with a form that is as culturally – and financially – vulnerable as poetry. The poet who goes by what she thinks she *should* write, paying more attention to fashion than to her own poetic identity, will never write anything that goes *beyond* that fashion.

A place to do your writing is among the most important of all touchstones. Life's never perfect: but it's good to find an environment in which to write that really works for you as a comfortable, inviting and yet serious workplace. For some people, that's a dedicated table in their bedroom; for others, a desk in a window. For me, it's a shed. It needn't be spacious. That's often impossible, especially in an urban or family home. Instead it could be a favourite armchair – in which you settle with a board like a TV-dinner tray, or your laptop – where you can immerse yourself. Or it might be the kitchen table, ritually scrubbed down once a week, after everyone else has gone to bed. Best of all is to find, or create, a space that isn't shared with any of your other activities. Pick an armchair, if you normally curl up on the sofa with the kids, or put a table in that spare bedroom where no one goes except to do the ironing. Make this place inviting and mark it out for poetry, with the right number of cushions to support your back and with all your significant postcards and books close at hand. Then you know that the moment you sit down, you can get straight to the poetry.

Picking a writing table, or chair, is a form of domestic magic. Ascribing functions to a spot is close to ascribing powers to it. What you're really saying is, 'This is where I can do writing.' No wonder the Bardic Thrones awarded in Welsh Eisteddfodau are highly decorated! Being able to get straight down to poetry, without having to work out what you need and then create that space each day, is as close as most of us get to remaining with the work at all times. Yet, ideally, poetry would be a continuous strand of every poet's life, simply coming to the fore or moving into the background at certain moments. Its way of thinking, and the deepening project of working it out in poem after poem, would accompany the writer through every part of his life, influencing and being influenced by them.

If the stakes for poetry really are as high as the example of Rilke seems to suggest, perhaps it's not unreasonable to look at how the contemplative life organizes itself. In most traditions, formal prayer isn't continuous but takes place at set times of day, between bouts of practical labour such as farming, sewing or even the management of religious communities. Prayer or contemplation continue *through* these other tasks, and are said to be changed by and to change them. Such continuity is really important for poetry too. A process that continually stops and starts has to keep 'reinventing the wheel', both in the making of one particular poem and more generally. One of the reasons that MA courses in creative writing are so attractive to emerging poets is that they allow students a year's *uninterrupted* concentration on their writing: a year in which they can put it first, building everything around what the university tells them their writing needs. Such sustained attention – even leaving aside the guidance of tutors – allows the student writer to bring all of her skills and character to bear on her work. Yet, in Britain at least, professional poets rarely have such liberty. This is both a loss – we must have missed out on much wonderful work that never had the chance to get written – and an encouraging model. It *is* possible to produce a body of poetry without the privilege of long periods of dedicated time.

Most important in making this happen, though, are personal qualities *beyond* your actual talent for poetry. You need ingenuity, determination and a strong working vision of what you believe poetry to be. While determination may be just the outward manifestation of that strong vision – a certainty about which direction to head in, at least for the moment – ingenuity plays across the whole of poetry practice. As we'll see when we look at formal models later on, it's what puts the play into poetics. It solves technical problems and turns lifeless lumps of verse into living poems. Ingenuity allows poetry to find new ways of working: to pre-empt the predictable and make the case for the exceptional. It is also, though, what devises strategies that allow the poet to carve time out of their busy week to write; to gain access to a role model despite the impossibility of doing so through a depleted public library service; to find guidance even in the absence of tutors, mentors or editors.

On the page, at least, the poet has more in common with such trickster figures as Jack in the Green or Coyote than with the author of scholarly work, reportage or genre fiction writing. 'Poetry is what's lost in translation', Robert Frost famously said. A more useful way to say this might be that poetry's what's lost in paraphrase. To write a synopsis of a poem is to lose its uniqueness. Line by line, poems defy the grammar-correct function in Microsoft Word. They refuse to respect the right-hand margin of the blank page. They're not objective or factual – or even reliable as autobiographical statements. The truth they tell is, as the American metaphysical poet Emily Dickinson says, 'slant'. Poetry is predictable only according to its *own* logic. In other words, ingenuity is another term for poetic self-reliance.

Here's the Victorian artist and cultural critic John Ruskin on the 'characteristic or moral elements' of Gothic art and craft: an architectural tradition he maintains is achieved by *individual creativity* among stonemasons and carpenters, rather than in schematic planning by a single architect or mass-produced design:

> As belonging to the builder, they would be expressed thus: –
> 1. Savageness or rudeness. 2. Love of Change. 3. Love of
> Nature. 4. Disturbed Imagination. 5. Obstinacy. 6. Generosity.

This is worth stealing as an evocation of the vitality and inventiveness of the poetic process. Of course, it doesn't mean that the emerging poet has nothing to learn. On the contrary, poetry contains a body of techniques and strategies to allow what the individual writer has to offer to emerge.

That's what this book is for. If you follow it chapter by chapter, it will build up into a poetry-writing course that allows you to experiment and find the whole range of your own writing. This potential range is nearly always larger than your starting point, whatever that may have been. Poets develop! The chapters that follow offer you not only insights into specific genres, but more general approaches and techniques: some to use at all times, some for when other strategies aren't working. You can also 'hit and run' specific chapters, especially if you've already been writing for a while and feel you just need help with specific topics. Finally, this book itself should be a *vade-mecum*. You should be able to turn to it for support and encouragement when the poetic going gets tough. Not everybody is lucky enough to secure a mentor – especially in the early stages of their poetry journey, when they most need one. A book is no substitute for a live poet reading your own work, but it *is* a resource. Use it as such.

As this chapter has suggested, it's also important to use your *own* resources: your touchstones, your writing place, your sense of poetry as forming part of who you are at all times. And one more thing – touchstones remind you how you came into poetry and what it means to you. You can distil this by creating a definition of poetry: what it means to you and what you aim to write. You'll probably need to work at this a little, drafting it down from a brainstorming exercise to a single sentence. Set aside a writing session to do so.

You're not aiming here for a watertight, lexicographer's definition of the kind that answers the question 'How do I know it's not prose?' but something much more aspirational. It might include your own symbolic shorthand. If, like William Blake, you use the sunflower as a personal symbol for joy, your definition might conceivably go: 'Poetry is a marriage of sunflowers and rhythm' – though that might equally make you feel embarrassed! There may also be images that fix the range or register you want your work to speak out of: 'Poetry speaks for *both* the processing plant Mum worked in *and* the British Library'. Images are useful fixatives. And this is, in fact, a *resolution* you're making: to try to write in a way you believe in. So it probably needs all the fixatives it can get. But you can also use abstracts: 'Poetry is concise beauty'. You can even steal another poet's definition if you feel it truly encapsulates what you want to say – once you've worked through your *own* drafting process.

The definition you pick can, and probably will, change over time. But for now it's shorthand for everything you hope for from your writing. As such it should live in your wallet, by your computer, or on your fridge door. If you're in a real hurry, you can even change it into an explicit resolution: *'I'm writing poetry that speaks for both the processing plant Mum worked in and the British Library'*; *'My poetry is the marriage of sunflowers and rhythm'*; *'My poetry is concise and beautiful'*. You can even repeat it to yourself as an affirmation. Repeat it half a dozen times, while you brush your teeth or do some other regular task, so that it becomes a habit of thought.

2 Going in: finding and using your material

And what rough beast, its hour come at last,
Slouches towards Bethlehem to be born?

> W.B. Yeats, 'The Second Coming'

Poetry looks both inwards and outwards. My writing table is below a window: in fact, it's surrounded by windows, since I work in a garden shed. Shed and garden are surrounded in turn by fields. Prairie-farmed, flat, often muddy, these are very much a workplace, just like my shed. Agro-industrial plant roll up and down to a nearby drying hangar. The shed walls are thin and the steps of birds on its felt roof sound like giant hooves.

But this seems to me a good position to be in. I'm enclosed by – and *from* – the landscape. I can observe it at times: and ignore it at others. This kind of selection is something that poetry is particularly good at. In fact we could say that poetry *is* measure: *both* in the old sense of a line of music *and* in the wider sense that it juxtaposes and allocates, choosing to take so much of one element and a little more of another in order to create a distinctive mixture.

To put it another way, poetry measures out both form and content. This doesn't make it either systematic or predictable for the reader, but it does mean that, for the writer, pattern and proportion are part of the trick of it. It's like juggling, or

17

balancing: a poem that's too emotional for its material is embarrassing and indigestible. One that's too cool is unengaging. A poem that slips in and out of form makes the ear stumble over its own expectations like someone who hasn't yet got their sea legs. . . . And, after all, measure can be pleasurable. The American poet C.K. Williams, who often writes from human incident and its psychological story – in other words, from using *character* voice, which is close to speech – says that you can't write a poem until you've got its music. This is true. It's also scary, because music seems as though it might be an open field. Some poets prefer to count the beats, at least. In fact, many are almost numerologists. They count stanzas, lines, rhymes, beats, syllables and even vowels: as if a poem had a secret algebra that allowed them to 'get it right'.

Perhaps writer's block is the poetry equivalent of stage fright. Almost all good poets fear, at one point or another, that they'll never write well again. It's not surprising that they should hope to find a winning formula, such as the number of feet in a line or the total of stanzas in a poem, that would guarantee they could continue. But long before this kind of professional superstition comes the straightforward pleasure of using a recipe to build a poem, and this is open to all. The Anglo-Welsh poet Gillian Clarke used to take a Wish Bag to her schools' workshops. This canvas sack held a piece of driftwood, an owl's feather, a flint – and so on. A child only had to pick one of these magically evocative objects for a poem to start to form. Once he had an observation from each one of his senses about his chosen object, the main ingredients of a simple poem were in place. What does this show us? Well, it suggests that one object + 5 senses = a riddle. Such a formula seems almost poetic in itself. Arguably, there are quite a few current in British poetry today. For example: period brand name + anecdote + note of longing = nostalgia poem. Myth + political reading + heroic couplets = one for the intellectual canon; 1 scientific fact + 2 effects of the light + 3 colours = the laboratory lyric. 'Thirteen Ways of Looking at a Blackbird' = a poem by Wallace Stevens. 'Fourteen Ways of Touching the Peter' = a poem by George MacBeth. . . .

This is mischievous. But such formulae, although they're half-game, half-absurdist-checklist, *can* be serious aids to poem-making, providing you discard them early in the process. They demystify poem-building and so, in a sense, the whole question of what a poem is. Once you've read a certain amount of poetry from any one time and place (other countries and centuries have literary fashions too!), you'll be able to identify some in actual use. Try analysing two or three poems that you've especially enjoyed. How would you formulate each? Try dreaming up a few ideal – or ridiculous – formulae. You could even write a poem using one of them.

The idea of using a measure of one thing and something of another, with all that it suggests about the way a poet *chooses* content, is also a good accompaniment to exploring your own poetic material. It grounds that exploration, and makes it manageable. Measure allows you to simply *select* poetic material, without worrying too much about how to express it, marry it up or even get all of it in.

So what *is* poetic material? It's the internal reality that produces your poems. That's not simply the life of the emotions (and it's certainly not a set of symptoms: poetry isn't the same as therapy). Nor is it just the unconscious, which we might assume to be rich and incomprehensible but out of reach. Poetic material *is* partly made up of these psychic elements, but it also includes preoccupations, hobby-horses, world-view, cultural background – and beliefs about poetry. It's the *why* of writing: which produces the *which*. The English poet Peter Redgrove's 'formula' for a true poem asked the writer to use the whole quartet of senses, emotion, intellect and intuition. It remains one of the most challenging, and at the same time accurate, definitions of poetry that we have.

A great deal of poetry today is written in workshops. These are great places to think about the craft of poetry, and to work out what does and doesn't work. But a new poem written in

19

response to a writing exercise is likely – unless the timing's very lucky – to be occasional verse. That's to say, it's verse written on a particular occasion, to an arbitrary, external stimulus. As a result, it may lack the living poetic matter that internal necessity generates. Poetry, since it looks both out and in, has to be *about* something in order to be fully *present*. That doesn't mean it must be intellectually driven, or politically engaged, or that its meaning is somewhere beyond the poem itself, in a cultural situation or emotional climate that the poem can 'help us to understand'. But it does mean that the poem is *exploring something*: even if that 'something' is simply its own form, as is the case with such famous poetic games-players as Gertrude Stein or the automatic-writing Surrealists.

Contrary to popular belief, poems very rarely do nothing except describe a 'sweet, especial rural scene', as Gerard Manley Hopkins's poem 'Binsey Poplars' has it. William Wordsworth's 'Daffodils', one of the most traduced poems in the English Romantic tradition, is in fact about the nature of experience: about *what it is like to remember* his 'host of golden daffodils', how 'They flash upon the inward eye / That is the bliss of solitude'. And even descriptive poetry is always more than a mere record. A poem is never a holiday snap. Instead, poetic material is a mixture of emotion, observation, insight, preoccupation. It is, in short, a mixture of elements very much like the self who writes. The Czech poet Miroslav Holub's 'A Boy's Head' charms us because of the utterly characteristic and at the same time idiosyncratic things he lists as occupying the boy's mind, starting with ' . . . a spaceship / and a project / for doing away with piano lessons'. The British poet Christopher Reid has a pastiche 'Central European' poem, written in the persona of *Katerina Brac*, which works in a similar way. His 'The Box' includes 'a message received from a friend of a friend / a journey by train, an odd-looking parcel'. This 'list of ingredients' makes a poem in almost the same way as our formulae did. It seems unlikely that these things will add up, yet they do.

Peter Redgrove's crossroads of forces also reminds us how

the *full range* of who you are must be brought to bear in poetry. After all, if a poem is, as T.S. Eliot says in 'East Coker', a 'raid on the inarticulate' – which is to say if it is at all mysterious, going further than what we think we know – it certainly can't know less than its author. A good poem is more than the sum of its own parts: and it must be more than the sum of the poet's parts too.

Isn't this hard to achieve? Well, yes. Writing real poems *is* hard. If it were easy, poems would be two-a-penny. They're not. James Joyce's early collection, *Pomes Penyach*, has a title that deliberately subverts the very nature of poetry. Poems *are*, in some way, special – but that doesn't mean that writing poetry is an elite activity, or the product of an expensive education. *Everybody* can go a little further into their own psyches than they do in day-to-day routine. Everybody can dream, feel, observe and understand: and choose to put these things together. Everybody can learn to pay attention to their freshest thoughts and instinctive insights: honouring their own particular way of seeing the world. One of the most striking poetry workshops I've ever led was held weekly in a day centre for adults with learning difficulties. For eighteen months, a group of women – only one with any degree of literacy, the majority with basic difficulties with language, such as with sentence-formation – met to produce poems, stories, riddles, and even re-told myth. Here, for example, is their 'World Tree', after the Norse myth of Yggdrasil:

Perhaps the world isn't a round ball.
Perhaps it's a tree.
The roots go down to the underworld
where anger and hate and criminals and murderers are;
and the branches go up to heaven
where God and the angels are.
That would mean that everything is joined
to everything else;
that the world is a place
where good and bad are joined.

21

Writing poetry is *not*, despite the way some opportunities for participation seem to have been put together, a competition. Instead, it means being in a particular relationship to your *own* capacities. This book is about establishing that relationship. It does not tell you what kind of poems you should write – because you will find your own poems, and nobody else's, through doing these things. Like other significant relationships, this one is going to be both private and idiosyncratic. All the same, you're going to have things in common with other writers' processes. Luckily – writers being who they are – the literature is full of clues about these.

In his famous definition of Negative Capability, from a letter to his brothers in 1817, John Keats talks about the poet as 'capable of being in uncertainties, Mysteries, doubts, without any irritable reaching after fact & reason'. Yet he certainly *finished* poems. He wasn't advocating writerly indecision but, rather, a profound openness to possibilities that might occur within the writing process. To begin with – to create the habit – it may help to think of this in more active terms. The starting point for a poem must be a place where *everything* is thinkable. There can be no thought police at the source of writing. Small wonder freedom of expression is so fiercely (or is it haplessly?) advocated by writers. Most of them aren't civil liberties heroes, or endowed with exceptional political acuity. They just know that, if something is forbidden in their work from the outset, the whole thing will be artificial – in the same way that occasional verse often is. It won't be driven by the full resource of their poetic material, but will involve *selection before expression*. Imagine driving with one eye shut. Not only do you lose a sweeping crescent of peripheral vision: you become unable to judge depth. Nothing could be worse for poetry.

Poets devize many ways of accessing the full range of their own material. All are strategies for getting round the internal censors: thought patterns that are excessively self-critical, or that demand a finished piece at the outset, or that rely on existing conventions as a guide for how to formulate text.

Internal censors cut off whole areas of material. Like all fixed patterns, they're among the most difficult of behaviours to shift. Fortunately, we do have role models for how to get past them.

Ted Hughes and Seamus Heaney, two poets who dominated British poetry in the late twentieth century – and still cast a long shadow today – each have a famous poem about how they access poetic material. In 'Digging' – and in the vertical, excavatory 'Bog Poems' of his second and third collections – Heaney digs down *from where he is* to find his own layers of meaning and resonance. He aspires to be workmanlike, immediate and concrete: 'But I've no spade to follow men like them'. Heaney's poems ask their speaker, *'Who are you?'* and, in starting from where he is, they are profoundly reflexive. Try asking yourself the same question, *'Who am I?'* Brainstorm it, using mind-maps or lists to turn the question round and ask it in different ways. What are the forms that identity can take for *you*? Who am I culturally? Emotionally? In my dreams and desires? As distinct from what other people think of me? When I try and describe myself in the third person? As expressed in my activities and possessions?

Ted Hughes's poem 'The Thought-Fox' pictures a radically different process, with the thought/poem/fox:

Coming about its own business

Till, with a sudden sharp hot stink of fox
It enters the dark hole of the head.
The window is starless still; the clock ticks,
The page is printed.

For this poet, the great effort is to get beyond the self to the given world, whether that's concrete (the vividly realized animal kingdom of *Moortown Diary* or *What is the Truth?*), emotional (as in the *Birthday Letters*, written in old age, about his tragic marriage to Sylvia Plath), or immaterial (as in some of his loosely spiritual poems about the monarchy, or constructing the *Crow* myth). Hughes's essay 'The Burnt Fox', tells us how the incidents of this famous poem really did happen; the idea for the poem seemed to 'enter' the poet's mind because he made himself open to it.

How to make yourself open like this? Poetry requires 'wool-gathering' – the kind of unfocused browsing and pottering that so irritates the people we live with. The poet doesn't know *what* she's looking for as she reads a couple of poems in a magazine, glances at the newspaper, wanders round the room picking things up and putting them down again. The metabolism of consciousness is mysterious. It is by nature prior to, and hidden from, the content of thought. Once you start to think, 'I'm creatively wool-gathering', your attention switches to yourself, you become self-conscious and the process stops. So this deliberate entry into a more spacious way of thinking has to get past self-consciousness – which always comes with an armoury of self-criticism and internalized conventions. Your entry into yourself is an attempt to duck the censors who stand at the gates of your consciousness telling you things like, 'You've nothing interesting to say', 'No one's going to read this', 'No thought but in rhyme', 'Watch your language' and, best of all, 'So-and-so doesn't do it like this'. Writing a poem and exposing it to a reader – whether that's an attentive partner or an anonymous print readership – is a risky thing to do. Self-consciousness knows this, and can make writing almost impossible.

One way to stop self-sabotage is to write poems 'in dialogue with' work you admire. I often do this. I may not know the poet I pick – who may be dead – but I feel the spark of recognition and ownership Eliot talks about in his essay 'Tradition and the Individual Talent'. For a few weeks or months, my poems will address a version of the *mind* I imagine is behind, and manifest in, someone's writing. This allows me not to write pastiche, but to pay attention to my chosen topics as if *by way of* the other poet. It's a bit like wearing a mask. It's also a bit like avoiding shyness, in a room where you don't know

24

anyone, by asking other people about themselves.

Some writers use music when they're writing, to set the tone of what they want to write *and* to occupy part of their attention. Music, after all, is a human language and it's almost impossible not to 'follow' it. Think how hard it is not to walk in time to a busker! Even if it's so familiar that you don't need to follow it, music can still absorb and preclude conscious, 'joined-up' thought. And it does a third thing: which is to raise the stakes. It's hard to write unmusically to a musical accompaniment – even if you're just making rough notes. That 'musicality' can make itself felt in a number of ways: as beauty, as containment within form, or as lyric 'flow'. Music means different things to different listeners but – providing it means neither too much nor too little to you – it may be worth seeing whether it will help you get past your own mental gatekeepers.

Some people write in cafés or other public places, where the 'white noise' of outer life can be enough to prevent self-consciousness. I rely on the view from my shed for this. I couldn't estimate what proportion of my writing time is spent looking up from the screen to the horses in the paddock, or formulating a phrase while I watch the willows move in their characteristic rhythm. One of the most persuasive advocates of the café writing table is Natalie Goldberg, whose inspirational *Writing Down the Bones* is built on the importance of free-writing – of 'going in' – as a practice, or repeated discipline.

The rule of free-writing is that there are no rules. But nevertheless, at least to begin with, the important thing is to keep the pen moving – which means without pausing to correct and without hesitating – for a set number of minutes. It's good to start with three minutes, because that's very manageable. As soon as that feels comfortable, or indeed too easy, you can try moving to five minutes, or seven. Use a stopwatch so you don't have to keep checking the time.

Free-writing is useful in a number of ways. First, it allows you to go into your material – which is to say, yourself – from where you *are*, rather than from where you *ought* to be. Second, it doesn't make you self-conscious about outcomes. Third, it allows – indeed forces – you to think in ways you couldn't have anticipated if you had been monitoring yourself. Free-writing doesn't produce final texts: what it does is to open the doorway to your own material. That door always opens both ways. Sometimes the trigger to writing is external, sometimes internal. When I do free-writing warm-up exercises in workshops, the group is usually divided equally between those who write about the room around them, almost like an observation exercise, and those who bring preoccupations with them. Most participants, but not all, write in the present tense. What's going on in your mind *right now* may actually be a memory, or anxiety about the future. Though it's not actually happening in the outer world, it *is* in the inner.

Some writers go still further over the threshold of consciousness, by practising forms of self-hypnosis. The poet Herbert Lomas lies on a sofa and talks himself down seven flights of imaginary stairs, along a visualized corridor and into the furthest room, where he lies down on a sofa and writes a poem. It's a technique he developed while teaching. He had almost no time to write and so *had* to make the little available to him work. Similarly, though few writers describe themselves (as did the composer Karl Heinz Stockhausen) as *transcribing* ethereal vibrations, several see writing poetry as a kind of shamanism. In Ted Hughes's 'The Thought-Fox', radical openness *invokes* the poetic Other.

Going in to your poetic material is a way to get closer to your *own* self, rather than the self who has written so far, or a version of you constructed by the people around you. At the same time it's an adventure, in which you go beyond external aspects in order to catch up with another, less familiar, version of your self. Poetry is always on the edge of stepping out into what you don't know: into a self you don't recognize, beyond the rational and comprehensible into more archaic forms of knowledge. Beyond this threshold are shapes that aren't yet recognizable: they might be trees, sociable or terrifying creatures, or half-recognized people. Your job is to observe them without getting carried away from the lighted room you need to write in. Poets, like poetry, need to look both ways.

3 Who goes there?
The poetic persona

Blest pair of Sirens, pledges of heaven's joy,
Sphere-born harmonious sisters, Voice, and Verse.
John Milton, 'At a Solemn Music'

To read a poet is often to develop a feeling of intimacy, or possessiveness. A reader who asks the author to sign their book is looking to symbolize that feeling. But what's given them such an impression of intimacy?

All writing has a 'speaking voice'. It's a form of dictation to that inner 'ear' which is the writer's, and reader's, *reading self*. Sometimes, this reading self is more impatient or critical than its owner would be in daily life. For example, I 'read' news stories, in newspapers or on the radio, much more critically than I would something a friend told me about her life. When I use an encyclopaedia, I skim ruthlessly past irrelevant paragraphs, or pause to browse something quite unrelated to what I was searching for. At the same time, when I read poetry that I enjoy, I do so like a jealous lover. I'm both trying to find the source of my enjoyment – what Michael Frayn, in his perceptive novel about writing, calls *The Trick Of It* – and hoping that there *is* no trick: that this *is* as good as it seems.

I also read with a strong sense of personal ownership: a

feeling that this writing can accompany and clarify my own experience. When I hear the Palestinian poet Mahmoud Darwish's *Jidiriyya*, an appeal against death by the very heart disease that killed him, I think there's no topic that so defines our humanity. Yet when I read Yehudi Amichai's love-poetry, I'm reminded of the importance of celebration.

The inner ear 'listens to' what we read in ways that are sometimes like those in which we listen to speech, and sometimes not. Writing itself understands this. Out of a rich plurality of possible words and ideas, it arranges itself into a single line of *address*. Elsewhere, literature calls this the *line of speech*. But there's nothing automatic about it. As Modernism showed in the first half of the twentieth century, it isn't the same as a *line of thought*. Virginia Woolf's stream-of-consciousness, in novels like *Mrs Dalloway*, isn't merely a special strategy for telling a story: it's an attempt to record the experience of consciousness itself, in all its *non*-linearity and multiplicity. After all, our thinking selves are at least partly verbal. Making yes/no statements, finding names for things – the attempt at symbol formation, however chaotic – arrives early, as Aristotle pointed out, and stays late, even in advanced Alzheimer's disease.

And yet our thinking selves use language in the non-unitary, non-linear ways that Woolf, Joyce and others portrayed. When we think, we're generally aware of more than one thing at once; and the ideas that occupy us may be unrelated in either content or register. For example, as I write this I'm aware of how cold my feet are; I worry whether my typing is disturbing a friend reading on the sofa behind me; the last paragraph has reminded me of a passage, from Woolf's *Mrs Dalloway*, about the despair of auto-didact Septimus Warren Smith; and I'm thinking about Paddington Station, where I first read *Mrs Dalloway*.

This multiplicity is perfectly normal. But writing, which wants to *confide* in the reader's inner ear as well as to *sustain itself* out loud, doesn't score simultaneous lines of thought, like a composer's orchestration. Nor does it leave them under-articulated, as a note to self. Instead, writing presents experiences or perceptions one after another, in a single *voice*.

It's this voice – a flexible concept but one widely used to think about and teach writing – that the reader has a relationship with. The mind's ear has no model for configuring voice, other than as belonging to a person. That's to say: when we read, we react *as if the text were a person*. The French cultural critic Roland Barthes put this the other way around when he pointed out, in *The Death of the Author*, that the author becomes reduced to a brand. We can hear this in a phrase such as 'Have you got the new Paul Muldoon?' Of course, the poet hasn't engineered a race of clones – it's his latest *book* that is new.

So to write is always to cultivate a persona. And this 'self on the page' may bear little resemblance to its author. Which is not to say that writing – including poetry, so often assumed to be straightforwardly confessional – is 'dishonest': a matter of constructions that are somehow 'out there' and have nothing to do with the true perceptions of the person who writes them. It may be more helpful to think of writing as a contrivance – like a mask, or puppetry – by which the writer shapes his or her ideas and experience into something that can address someone else: the reader. The Reverend Patrick Brontë encouraged his prodigious children to use a mask when they needed to talk to him about problems. He understood that it was a liberating device; and several commentators have speculated on its link with the development of their literary skills. Drama uses specific fictional roles and narratives to allow the audience a true experience of, for example, grief or pleasure.

One very immediate example of how to create a self on the page forms part of almost everyone's writing experience. You write to the bank manager very differently from how you'd email a friend. These manners aren't false; they simply exhibit different aspects of your personality. Each is a *persona*: the expression of some form of personality, in writing organized into a single voice. That's likely to be internally consistent in register or pitch: the letter to the bank manager shouldn't become abusive, and your email is unlikely to include formal greetings. And this coherence of register and pitch is one of the keys to consolidating a persona, which draws on its author's expertise to write *as if* it's authoritative, charming or happy, for example.

All writing – especially poetry, which is accompanied by relatively few external facts (little in a poem can be checked with an encyclopaedia, after all) – relies on the *apparently personal* contact between itself and the reader. In fact, this contact is really a contract, in which the reader undertakes to accept what the poem does, for its duration, and the poem undertakes to convince the reader of its own value. Of course, this contract isn't always observed. Most poets can name critics who refuse to pay attention to a poem in its own terms and proscribe it according to others (usually, their own): the formalist who rubbishes something just because it's free verse, for example. Unfortunately, there are also lots of poems that forget to honour their side of the bargain. They lose our confidence when they reveal technical hitches – like giving a glimpse of the wings at scene-changes – or seem uncertain as to what they really mean. But it's hard developing an authoritative persona, one so confident and charming that a reader will put his or her trust in you. So the rest of this chapter looks at simple ways to build confidence and fluency in adopting such personae.

First and most important is to *write as if*. This *as if* must primarily be *as if you're worth reading*. Write *as if you deserve to write*. Most poets, when they begin, oscillate between believing that every word, since it came to them *as a poem*, must be good, and feeling that their writing isn't good enough to show to even the proverbial best friend. That oscillation can be hard to manage, especially if you're working alone. But the truth is *always* somewhere in between. No story about a poet emerging fully formed with their very first verse is anything other than lazy journalism. The most interesting poets continue to grow and develop throughout their careers: think about the different phases in the writing lives of D.H. Lawrence or his fellow novelist-poet, Thomas Hardy. But even poets who emerge fully formed with their first *published* work have worked hard to get to that stage. Recently the British literary press made a lot of fuss about a poet whose first book had been taken on by a major publisher. He's been described as 'an unknown' – and if you were a keen reader going into a bookshop outside London, that's probably what he would have been to you. But that first book had been preceded by years of study, workshopping, competition entries, networking, public readings, magazine publication, even a pamphlet: indeed, it was already under consideration by a respected specialist publisher when it was snapped up.

So everyone's early poems deserve to be written, though at the same time this doesn't mean that they have to be – or indeed will be – perfect. They will just be themselves. But you write them *as a poet*, albeit an emerging one. The aims you established in Chapter 1, and the material you identified in Chapter 2, are the foundation stones of your persona. They are where you write from.

When it comes to poetry, what you say matters: in both senses. It matters that you have your say, and it matters that what you say is of interest to both you and your reader. For *you* are the authority in your own poem. This is what a poetic persona is. Whenever you feel that authority slipping away, refer to your poetic aims and then remind yourself that *you're* the person carrying them out. This isn't the same as believing that your poem will emerge perfect. It's not like believing you can walk through walls, but it *is* like believing you can walk. That belief isn't as automatic as we'd like to think – which is why we tend to rush into the comfort of totalizing beliefs: 'I'm no good' or 'I'm brilliant'. But each poem – cliché or no – is a journey. You have to put one word in front of another in order to go forward.

If you still have difficulty in writing from a sense of authority, a mantra can keep this in place. Although it feels artificial, it's worth repeating to yourself, ten times, before you start writing, 'I am a poet for whom poetry is' – whatever definition you arrived at in Chapter 2 – 'angels and dirt' or 'sunflowers and postage stamps', etc. Or you could make it simpler still: 'I am the authority in my own poem'. Pretty soon, particularly if you combine it with sitting down to work in your habitual writing place, this should be ingrained and you shouldn't need to repeat it.

As you continue to write, your poetic persona may change and develop. You may come to see poetry as more, or less, a matter of pure language than you originally did. You could become interested in the new, or in tradition. You might also, like many professional poets, adopt more than one persona at a time. Once the people in your life know that you write poetry, you could find yourself called upon, for example, to write occasional verse for birthdays or weddings.

All of this means that it's useful to practise changing personae on the page. A workshop exercise I often use is one I developed with a theatre company, whose actors wanted to move from improvisation to script-writing. In other words, they knew how to get in character – moving and feeling in a different way – but not necessarily how to do so with words. Yet one of the best ways to characterize, in *writing* fiction or drama, is through a character's actual speech.

To demonstrate this, I ask students to re-tell some story or incident *as* a particular character. A complicated story takes a long time to tell, and can overtake characterization as the focus of attention. So I ask workshop participants to think of one of their very earliest memories: those that are *not* family stories, but are very early 'snapshots', usually entirely visual. These sense 'pictures', from the ages of two or three, are non-narrative and often rather blurry. They really are what William Wordsworth calls *spots of time*: moments of experience, frequently recalled with no narrative context, let alone content. My own very early memories include: sitting on the kitchen step while my mother hangs out the washing; walking past those stumpy rose bushes that used to feature in suburban front gardens; putting my fingers in my ears when a lorry goes past. Each of these spots of time is absolutely unexceptional, yet at the same time highly characteristic of a time and place.

In order to do this exercise yourself, write down one of your own early snapshot memories. It should run to something like a paragraph. It doesn't matter whether you write in the present or past tense. Some people write looking back; others as if they were their infant self. Whichever you chose, next do the opposite. It doesn't matter that the memory's going to recede somewhat in this exercise: what's going to come to the fore is the voice telling it. Now rewrite from the point of view of an adult who must have been nearby: since no child of that age is ever entirely alone, even if their carer's asleep next-door. Next, retell that moment as an animal who could have been there too. Even in the absence of pets, there are always birds flying overhead, ladybirds, spiders . . . Now rewrite the memory in the voice of a picture-book or fairytale; or that of myth. Remember that this is still an exercise in *voice*, not in adding an ending to the story. It should be helping you to experience how easy it is to *choose* a persona. Finally, return to your own *poetic* persona and write a first draft of a poem in that voice.

A very different way to see how voice characterizes is to imitate speech rhythm. The best way to do this is to transcribe how people talk – verbatim. The point of this exercise isn't to paraphrase or summarize speech: it's the very turns of phrase, the repetitions and redundancies that a speaker uses, that characterize them. Unless you know shorthand, it's almost impossible to transcribe legibly fast enough to keep up with speech. But the *act* of transcription, even if the result is to some extent illegible, is a real discipline. It teaches you to pay attention to every word. A good way to practise this is to find a seat in a train, bus or café: somewhere where you can write without being disturbed but are within earshot of other people. It's best to do this with strangers, too, since if you try to listen to someone you know – members of the family chatting downstairs, for example – you'll probably be distracted by the *content* of what they're saying!

Tune in to one particular conversation, and especially to an individual speaker, and write down every word they say – for as long as you can. By the way, mobile phone calls don't really work for this exercise because the people you'll overhear are often speaking unidiomatically, either because their signal's not great or because they're self-conscious. TV and radio don't work either: broadcast speech has often been edited to make it fluent. You want your transcription to form a real record of the speaker's character when you read it back.

After you've done this for a while, you may find yourself transcribing in lines that correspond to the natural phrasal rhythms of the speech you're listening to. More of this in Chapter 5. Meanwhile, it's worth doing this exercise whenever you find your poetry getting a bit stuck, or mannered. That can be a sign that it's talking to itself rather than to a reader.

Most of all, however, transcription should help you to experience how *voice characterizes* persona. This works in reverse, too: persona can alter voice. If your self on the page adopts an authoritative persona, you'll find yourself writing things that are more confident (for example, definitive statements), ambitious (your vocabulary may include words you don't usually bother with) and insightful (your poems reach unexpected conclusions) than you might have anticipated. In the next chapter, we'll develop this authority with a more technical approach to rhythm and metre.

4 The drum kit: metre

A dance is a measured pace, as a verse is a measured speech.
Francis Bacon, 'The Advancement of Learning' BK2, Ch16, #3

Like any oral performer, the poet needs a rhythm section. Traditionally, the lyric line has been sustained by a regular metre: a bit like the beats in music, but with a tighter set of rules about what you can do with them.

When you record the patterns of actual speech, as you did in the last chapter, one of the things you may notice is how *percussive* that speech is. Language clatters with *starts* of words and of syllables. Some have additional definition, provided by consonants; but vowels can start a sentence, word or syllable, too. In this way, the sounds that language makes – the sounds a poet arranges into metre – are like the notes of music. Written music marks where notes *start* within a rhythmic context (it also notes their duration: but that notation is given *at the start of* the note). Metre makes patterns out of the ways in which the parts of words *fall* in particular rhythms and patterns of stress. The stressed syllables in language operate as rhythmic centres of gravity in the same way as strong beats, or the starts of bars, in music. The trick of formal metre is to align these linguistic stresses into regularity, so that the line of poetry makes a regular sound.

Just like basic rhythms in music – three time, four time and the combination which is seven time – many of these formal metres have been part of the traditions that English-language poetry inherited since before the language itself existed. It is the Classical Latin and Greek tradition which generated this way of organizing poetry (we'll look at the influences of other traditions later). This Classical – which throughout history also meant literate, and so literary – tradition generated longer lines than the vernacular forms running alongside it. Compare the short lines and mixed metre of an anonymous mid- or late-fourteenth-century carol, which opens:

Jesu Christ, my lemmon [lover] swete,
That diyedest on the Rode Tree,
With all my might I thee beseche,
For thy woundes two and three . . .

with the long, regular lines that open Geoffrey Chaucer's book-length poem *Troilus and Criseyde*:

The double sorwe of Troilus to tellen,
That was the kyng Priamus sone of Troye,
In lovynge, how his aventures fellen
Fro wo to wele, and after out of joie . . .

Despite their very specific origins, it's worthwhile learning how to use strict metre for a number of reasons. First, it makes reading poetry a great deal more enjoyable when you can understand and name what's going on and why it works so well. Second, these metres do help to carry a poem onward. One of the things children find so enjoyable about making up doggerel is being able to fill in the rhythmic gaps with the first thing that comes to mind – and still have something that works. Of course, it may work as verse rather than as poetry: but that's another question. W.H. Auden said that poetry should be memorable, by which he also meant memorizable. Regular metrical poetry certainly *is* easier to memorize. It works a bit like predictive text. The demands of form close down options as the line goes on, till by the time you get to the clincher rhyme you can often guess what it is. While, if you already know the poem, the rhyme acts as a prompt.

A third reason for practising these disciplines is that several key forms in the Western tradition – not only the sonnet, but other Romance forms, such as the villanelle and sestina, which no serious emerging poet should exclude themselves from – cannot be written without a mastery of strict metre. Fourth and most important, skill in using strict metre is not only a precursor to any creative play with those metres, but a fundamental building block of poetic skill in *every* form, including free-verse. Something holds free-verse together, and it's not only the beauty of the ideas or clarity of the images. Something makes it into verse rather than 'poetic' prose – and that 'something' is internal tension, a structured sound, aural form. Once you know the grammar of rhythm – the names of metres and how they work – it's easy to 'read' any poem, including free-verse, for those rhythms, and to see its motors. Rhythm propels music: it does just the same in poetry. Without rhythm there is no movement, only stasis.

These motors aren't concealed, but they are embedded. Reading rhythmic form means going into the thick of a poem, as if you're hearing it speak from the inside. Working out a metre is like listening in as the poet works it out in their own head, line by line and phrase by phrase. This is a great way to 'own' a poem you've always admired; and, like artists drawing the works of great masters in order to learn how they do it, reading the metres of wonderful poems provides you with skills which, even if you don't *consciously* apply them, go straight into the building of your own poems.

The best way into the vocabulary of metre is through that most well known of forms, *iambic pentameter*. It's still the basic unit of much English-language verse, and the decent walking rhythm that characterizes many of its most famous lines, from Shakespeare – 'Shall I compare thee to a summer's day?' – to Tony Harrison's epigraph, from his famous poem about graveyard graffiti, *V*: '*Beneath your feet's a poet, then a pit. /*

Poetry supporter if you're here to find how poems can grow from
(beat you to it!) SHIT / *find the beef, the beer, the bread, then look behind.'*

The term itself, though, is a compound. *Metre* refers to the number of stresses in a line. Pentameter, like the five-pointed pentagram, has five; hexameter has six. Quatrameter, less common, has four. In fact, scansion doesn't count stresses, but feet. But a foot has a stress in it – in fact, it is led and defined by its stress (even though the stress may not come at the start of the foot). It is the ear, rather than the eye, that tells where feet fall in a line.

Listening to where a stress falls in a word is the opposite of technical. We all hear the distortion in a recording where words have been spliced together so that the music of a sentence is all wrong: the pause before the name of a station in a train arrival announcement; or the wrong inflection in a recorded apology. This is much more sophisticated than simply knowing where the stress in a word goes, although non-native speakers with the finest of ears can still get caught out, particularly by English irregularity, on place names and other proper names. Try putting the stress on, say, the last syllable of a few of these and you quickly realize how strongly the ear resists an inaccurate stress: Bolton, Paddington, Cardiff, Edinburgh. In fact, very often the stress is the motor within a word, particularly if that word is fairly long: try saying 'photosynthesis' or 'antidisestablishmentarianism' with displaced stress and you'll find yourself lost among the syllables.

Reading for stress doesn't need to be too careful: it's often easiest to hear when you say a line quite quickly and casually. This is the skeleton of rhythm; it's what remains when everything else is stripped away. First lines are often especially clear. Open any anthology at random and you find, respectively, four-, five- and six-stress lines almost shouting at you: 'Long-expected one-and-twenty' – Samuel Johnson, 'A Short Song of Congratulation'; 'Thou still unravished bride of quietness, / Thou foster-child of Silence and slow Time' – John Keats, 'Ode on a Grecian Urn'; 'Sickness broke him. Impatient, he cursed at first, but mended' – Gerard Manley Hopkins, 'Felix Randal'.

However, that last poem opens with a six-stress line of a different kind: 'Felix Randal the farrier, O is he dead then? My duty all ended'. And here's a five-stress line that isn't true pentameter – 'Go, for they call you, shepherd, from the hill' – opening Matthew Arnold's 'The Scholar Gypsy'. Clearly, something more complex is going on here. Expectation is being subverted, for pentameter, hexameter and their cousins of different lengths generally name a *regularly* occurring stress in a line. They say, in effect: these are five beats of a particular kind of metre. One such particular beat, or foot, is the 'iamb' of 'iambic pentameter'.

Let's return to those sonnet openings. Their feet go weak-strong, weak-strong, as in the opening of Shakespeare's Sonnet 18:

> Shall I compare thee to a summer's day?
> Thou art more lovely and more temperate:
> Rough winds do shake the darling buds of May
> And summer's lease hath all too short a date:

In every line, weak-strong tramps five times across the page. It sounds like the march of reason; in a love-sonnet, this makes whim seem unarguable. The first rule of rhetoric – that you must sound convincing – is satisfied every time. Take John Milton's despair 'On His Blindness': 'When I consider how my light is spent ere half my days in this dark world and wide, and that one Talent which is death to hide lodged with me useless. . .' . Now put in the line-breaks, and the iambic pentameter – which is what makes this sound so clenched and passionate – becomes apparent:

> When I consider how my light is spent,
>   Ere half my days in this dark world and wide,
>   And that one Talent which is death to hide
>   Lodg'd with me useless, though my Soul more bent

To serve therewith my Maker, and present
My true account, lest he returning chide,
Doth God exact day-payment, light deny'd?
I fondly ask . . .

Iambic pentameter is so irresistible that it's everywhere, like a default setting of the ear. *Ottava rima*, where no metre is named, consists of eight-line stanzas of iambic pentameter rhyming, in a pattern that underlines rhythmic certainty with repetition, *ababcc*. *Blank verse*, the verse of Milton's *Paradise Lost* and Shakespeare's plays, is iambic pentameter that does-n't rhyme. Generally, however, since iambic pentameter developed its hold on English-language poetry at a time when rhyme was the norm, rhyme is assumed, though not named, by the term. Nevertheless, that rhyme was frequently sustained by complex patterning over whole stanzas or even poems. Consecutive lines didn't necessarily rhyme with one another: to do so would be conspicuously powerful because of the already-forceful nature of the metre. Small wonder, then, that when on rare occasions a couplet of consecutive lines in iambic pentameter rhymed, this became known as a *heroic couplet*.

Much contemporary 'free-verse' is in fact blank verse. Here is the opening of 'Dead March', one of Andrew Motion's elegies for his mother:

It's twenty years (*it's not, it's twenty-three –*
be accurate) since you were whisked away
(*I wasn't 'whisked away': I broke my skull*)

Ignore the dialogue and count the feet. Or, alternatively, listen to the dialogue and, when you're surprised at how well it fits the ear, hear this as the work the metre does. In fact, poets have had to try so hard not to be hypnotized by the march of iambic pentameter that free-verse frequently has to struggle to build itself on different foundations. We will look at escape strategies in later chapters.

But there are alternatives. One is to build flexibility into pentameter. Like any technique, metre, once mastered, becomes so 'owned' – so much part of the way you think – that there's scope to play around with it. Rhythm affords huge scope for this kind of creative play. Indeed, *not* to play at all can leave the poem in danger of sounding like an exercise. *Rhythm leans against itself.* Just as syncopation makes jazz – and indeed much traditional music from, in particular, Eastern Europe and the Middle East – come alive, an extra or dropped syllable can refresh the regular pulse of metre. So, especially where it underlines meaning – at a place where the narrative of a poem 'turns', or emphasis is required, for example – a line can be strengthened by changing one iamb for another kind of foot, as in those opening lines by Arnold and Hopkins. Of course, it's important not to do this too often, or else line and poem simply sound uncontrolled. Nor should a poem change wholesale from one regular metre to another halfway through. That just suggests loss of control, and the poem loses its identity. It's like poor continuity in a film: when the midnight car chase rounds a corner into bright sunshine, the contract of belief has been broken. Of course, this doesn't apply to a poem with section-breaks. Those breaks are just like the change of scene in a film: shifting what we see and also, often, mood and pace.

One of the most common variants of iambic pentameter keeps the iambs but adds a foot: an *alexandrine* is a line of iambic hexameter, which often ends a pentameter poem or stanza. That extra length allows a sense of conclusion: of arrival. In fact, a *Spenserian stanza* regularizes the appearance of the alexandrine, using one to make a ninth line at the end of each stanza in an otherwise iambic pentameter. There's a regular rhyme scheme, too: *ababbcbcc*. So strong is the authority of iambic metre that an alexandrine often passes almost unnoticed. Here's a stanza of the original, from Canto I of Edmund Spenser, *The Faerie Queen*, the incomplete epic for which he invented the form and which relies on the 'give' of the alexandrine as a form of propulsion. This whole stanza is a parenthetical description of the gentleness with which the knight kills his dragon:

As gentle Shepheard in sweete even-tide,
   When ruddy *Phoebus* gins to welke in west,
   High on an hill, his flocke to vewen wide,
   Markes which do byte their hasty supper best;
   A cloud of combrous gnattes do him molest,
   All striving to infixe their feeble stings,
   That from their noyance he no where can rest,
   But with his clownish hands their tender wings
He brusheth oft, and oft doth mar their murmurings.

Metre regularizes and solidifies the thought or image a poem offers the reader. It fixes it, which is perhaps one of the reasons why some poets, as we saw in Chapter 1, have called the poem 'a machine'. This returns us to the close alliance between metre and the memorizability of a poem. Evidence of this necessary relationship is built into the earliest poetry in English. *Kennings*, or noun compounds made from some kind of description, whether metaphor or concrete imagery, are used throughout Anglo-Saxon poetry – to our ears sometimes inelegantly and certainly opportunistically – to make up the metre. Often half-line phrases (the basic metrical unit in that poetry), they could be deployed if the reciter got lost.

Traditionally, school-teachers have got pupils to memorize poems whose strong rhythmic momentum helps along the processes of recitation and remembering. Experiencing how metre keeps a poem in the mind is salutary, however, for *all* emerging poets. Some serious writers memorize a poem once a month or even once a week. The result is a mental library of poems, but this exercise also produces a personal library of *sounds*. There's no better way to learn the effect of metre than to memorize a poem written in a particular form. If you plan to do this, I recommend starting with a sonnet in iambic pentameter: it fixes the metre in your mind and is a manageable length. Remember that repetition *after* the initial memorizing is what fixes a poem you've learnt. At first you'll need to repeat it more than once a day, then daily, then, after a while, weekly.

But there are many metres beyond the iambic. Formal English metres are known as *accentual-syllabic*, because they don't just count the number of stresses (accents) in a line, but build regular numbers of syllables around those stresses too. On the other hand, an *accentual* line, which could have its roots in accentual Anglo-Saxon formal verse, *only* counts accents. It often subverts the dignity of strict metre by cramming the rhythmically unexpected around these regular beats, as in these three-beat lines by Peter Reading:

> One who no longer *is*
> can't suffer – is merely the same
> as one who has never been.
> ('Lucretian')

A *syllabic* line counts only the number of syllables, regardless of stress. It is thus – to the ear, at least – an almost hidden discipline. Dylan Thomas was a surprising proponent. Poems such a 'In My Craft or Sullen Art' (with seven syllables in every line) and 'Poem in October' (where the syllable-counts for corresponding lines within each stanza broadly match) allow the sense of a much more fluid, singing voice than strict accentual-syllabic lines do, while still being tightly controlled.

There are also several other formal accentual-syllabic metres. The *trochaic* is composed of strong-weak *trochees*, as in words like 'shining' and 'water' – and it's the contagious metre of Henry Wadsworth Longfellow's infamous *Hiawatha*:

> By the shores of Gitche Gumee
> By the shining Big-Sea-Water
> Stood the wigwam of Nokomis,
> Daughter of the moon, Nokomis

. . . and so on, for hundreds of lines. The poem's clumsy colo-
nialism shouldn't distract us from the fact that Longfellow
was absorbing the still-equally primitive ethnography of his
day: in which the Finnish epic *Kalevala*, which also has a
trochaic rhythm, had just been assembled.

Dactylic metre, meanwhile, is built from *dactyls*, strong-
weak-weak feet. The most famous example is the opening of
Alfred Lord Tennyson's 'The Charge of the Light Brigade',
with its galloping 'Half a league, half a league, / Half a league
onward'. An *anapaest*, on the other hand, sounds weak-weak-
strong. Again, there's a famous nineteenth-century example –
Lord Byron's 'The Destruction of Sennacherib':

The Assyrian came down like the wolf on the fold
And his cohorts were gleaming in purple and gold;
And the sheen of their spears was like stars on the sea,
When the blue wave rolls nightly on deep Galilee.

These 'triplet' forms are fun to use, but they're so conspicuous
that to build whole lines of them is to offer hostages to
fortune. It's no coincidence that they were used with vigour
by the unabashed Victorians. Undiluted, though, they are the
opposite of cool: and the opposite of flexible, too, drowning
out the possibility of emotional subtlety and, indeed, range.

Finally, a *spondee*, made up of two strong beats, breaks the
pattern of beat-led metre more conspicuously than any other
foot. A poem written entirely in spondees is almost unimag-
inable: it would be relentless, like a megaphone ranter in place
of a string quartet. And spondees are rare: they are often made
up of two monosyllables, since a two-syllable word will
generally have a rhythmic inflection. Those monosyllables
have to be strong as nouns are. Conjunctions and articles, for
example, clearly fail the spondee test: 'The cat sat on the mat'
is *not* three spondees, even though it is made up of monosyl-
lables. A spondee is also confusing because, alone among the
forms, it seems to have two strong beats within a single foot.
It's useful, therefore, to fall back on the *quantitative* Classical

way of measuring feet from which English metre is derived, and to think of the spondee as two *long*, rather than 'strong', beats.

The extra weight it carries means a spondee, like a sort of rhythmic bouncer, can close a line with a degree of finality, just as an alexandrine will a poem. And this personification in turn reminds us that metres have traditionally been 'gendered'. A line that ends with a stress (like an iamb) has a *masculine ending*; one that ends with a weak syllable (such as its opposite, the trochee) has a *feminine ending*. As a woman poet myself, I probably don't need to spell out the complex of positive connotations that a 'masculine ending' has accrued: the note of arrival, the clear signpost, the tidy close. This means that trochees and dactyls build whole poems comparatively rarely; and, when they're used to vary the line, they don't do so at the break. The value attached to the strong closing syllable is of course entirely a matter of habit. The English ear is all at sea in the poetics of Romance, Slav and those other languages where stress is rarely placed on the final syllable of a word. But still, to use traditional metre is to enter a whole sound-scape, which must be congruent, so it's important to learn these patterns *before* choosing whether to abandon them.

Like all techniques, metre must become automatic to be any use in a *real* poem: one that *needs* to be written rather than something generated by an exercise. Simply memorizing the sounds isn't enough by itself. Metres, being infectious, want to move on and multiply. They demand to be practised. The best place to start is with blank verse – so avoiding the additional temptations and challenges of rhyme. This builds a strong sense of what we could call, after Douglas Dunn, the *Dante's Drum-kit* of iambic pentameter (though he uses the term in the specific context of *terza rima* – that is to say, along with the particular rhyme scheme of *The Divine Comedy*). Try this out. Simply start with an iambic pentameter line – about anything. Then try to answer it; then add another, and so on. It's surprising how often the pentameter line coincides with an entire phrase or thought.

Poetry, after all, has to be built as well as dreamt. Once you get underway, you can steer the emerging poem into exploration and evocation just as you usually do – while always keeping an ear on your diction. Very soon – exactly like riding a bike, on which you wobble only at the beginning – you'll find yourself producing blank verse without having to count the feet. Once you can do this, you're ready to introduce rhyme.

5 Beat into pulse

The force that through the green fuse drives the flower
Drives my green age;
        Dylan Thomas, 'The Force that through the Green Fuse
                                    Drives the Flower'

If metre is a way to measure and regulate – tightening up a
poem and drawing it together – then pulse is what brings that
rhythm, and the poem, alive. The pulse that ticks in my wrist
as I'm typing this, for example, is regular: but it's also organic,
intrinsic and spontaneous. When I'm nervous, or excited, it
races. If it were to slow down too much, I'd become inert –
and eventually die. The same is true of pulse in poetry. The
relationship between words and the rhythm in which they
sound – *the way they sound* – is one of mutual dependency. For,
while words map out and furnish a metre, they also depend
on it for impact and mobility.

Try reading anything aloud, and your sense of it changes.
That's equally true of textbook jargon and of the sonnet which
you've just memorized. (Indeed, I'd argue that it's impossible
to memorize a poem *without* saying it out loud, even if you do
so under your breath.) Actors talk about 'scoring' a play, by
which they mean establishing the through-rhythm in which
they take their turns and pace their words. The whole drama
must 'flow' in the same way as any other single piece, such as
a piece of music. Reading aloud isn't just a case of how the

vowels and consonants sit in the mouth, whether they clash or are a pleasure to articulate. It's also a question of cadence: the rise and fall of music and meaning, and the way writing records that rise and fall through punctuation and, in the case of poetry, lineation.

Intrinsic to the cadence of *this* prose, for example, is how far my concentration extends: how much 'idea' I can carry in my mind at any one time. Also impinging on it is my sense of the approximate length of every chapter and the way I'm dividing up my material. I have an idea of you the reader, too, as someone who needs clarity from this book – but has no desire to be patronized. There's also the rhythm imposed by paragraphs. They're a kind of necessary breathing-space. I rely on them to make the writing digestible for both of us. Finally, there's the way *register* – degree of intensity and sense of occasion – impinges on my rhetoric. Because I have a sense of occasion that is *both* discursive *and* teacherly as I write this, I'm tending to use longer, more rolling sentences than I might in, for example, a travel piece. It's true that I also use quite long sentences when I write reviews. Their orotundity makes me feel authoritative. But they're a temptation, too, since they make statement – and overstatement – easy. Long sentences don't encourage precision. I admit I'd use a different tone in an email, even if I were commenting on the very same book.

So scoring, cadence and register, all of which are at work in writing, form a poem's pulse. Even while it's being written, that pulse contains at least a trace of the future poem's identity. Indeed, one of the hardest things about working through numerous drafts is that, if the eventual poem assumes a very different form, or even focus, from that of the original, its existing music may suddenly fail to fit it. The logic of *pulse* is a deep structure, and it's one of the ways we instinctively judge whether a poem is 'authentic': by which we probably mean authentic *to itself*, since a poem, after all, doesn't have to be 'true to' its author's life.

One thing transcribing speech patterns may have shown up is the way those patterns characterize *through being predictive.*

Once you have someone's voice in your inner ear, you can reproduce the way that person is likely to speak before they even open their mouth. Traditional TV comedy script-writers, hung up on catchphrases, got this partly wrong. Predictive pattern has much more to do with speech *rhythm* than with any particular turn of phrase. But, just as one line of formal metre entails another, so one phrase, in any given pattern of speech, can entail the next. If you've ever caught yourself 'carrying on', whether in an argument or while trying to articulate just how bad that day at the office was, you'll recognize the sensation of hearing your own repetitions go on as if on automatic pilot: as if each phrase somehow *generated* the next without your even thinking about it.

According to the French philosopher and psychoanalyst Julia Kristeva, what's involuntary – in other words, emotional – gets reflected in a sudden upsurge in the musical elements of speech. These are sound effects – rather than bearers of meaning – such as stammering, repetition and intensified cadence. Of course, they do convey *emotional* meaning, and this musicality is part of how poetry operates. Poetry co-opts the music of emotion, which can be heard first of all in the way rhythmic phrases balance each other. Listen to how, in free-verse couplets, the lines seem to *entail* each other. Here's the opening of Alice Oswald's 'Hymn to Iris':

> Quick-moving goddess of the rainbow
> You whose being is only an afterglow of a passing-through

And here's the whole of 'Corinna' by Michael Longley:

> Have you fallen asleep for ever, Corinna?
> In the past you were never the one to lie in.

Now, here are three first lines. You don't know what's coming next – and yet you can probably imagine the way each continues *rhythmically*:

For the first time in a long time

And:

The bead-cold eyes of the Great Blue Heron

And:

Like coming late to a tough public school.

Here's how each does in fact continue:

> For the first time in a long time
> there is sun making sunshine,
> > (Bill Manhire, 'Song')

> The bead-cold eyes of the Great Blue Heron
> > That should be called the Great Grey
> > > (Greg Delanty, 'The Natural World')

> Like coming late to a tough public school.
> They all know the rules except me
> > (U.A. Fanthorpe, 'Terminal Feelings')

By itself, rhythmic balance is a crude tool. Poetry, like speech, relies on a more subtle interplay of forces to characterize it than simple rhetorical *momentum*. Of these, perhaps the most self-contained is register. Certain formal metres, such as spondees, are 'louder' – more emphatic and blunter – than the decorations and qualifications permitted by unstressed syllables in other feet. For example, *The cat sat on the mat*, with its three iambs, occupies a completely other register from *Was the cat on the mat?* spoken as a pair of anapaests.

Choices of register, which may cut across cadence, are also important in lineation. Poets tend to avoid weaker words at either end of lines: articles and, usually, prepositions and conjunctions, don't easily bear the weight of lines of verse, because they don't generally bear the weight of clauses: curses ending in 'off' are an exception, and the more striking because of it! Phrases that shuttle between one weak word and another sound inconclusive and unsettled: we want them to *arrive* somewhere.

Try mis-lineating any verse and saying it out loud:

In living rooms where fathers
sprawl, still
clothed, the bumpy core beyond
Sinatra's voice beats inside a radiogram, a
pulse deep
under. There's rain on the
windows.

Rather than:

In living rooms where fathers sprawl, still clothed,
The bumpy core beyond Sinatra's voice
Beats inside a radiogram, a pulse
Deep under. There's rain on the windows.

(Paul Farley, 'The Sleep of Estates')

Correctly lineated, the poem comes clear. One way to get a feel for this is to take a couple of poems by a poet you admire, someone rhythmically straightforward – say the Seamus Heaney of *Seeing Things* – and cover up the ends of the lines with your hand, or a sheet of paper. You can more or less guess the last word of each because of how organically it fits the poem. It will nearly always be a noun or verb. You can also cover the left-hand margin to do the same with first words. Both first and last words are the agents of a line – indeed of a whole poem. They muscle it along, rhythmically and semantically. To practise further, Google a poet you admire, and download a couple of poems you don't know at all well. Working quickly, so you don't get to know the poems, paste each one into a paragraph. How accurately can you re-insert the line-breaks?

Another way to modulate what you say is with punctuation, which can break up a line and alter its character without affecting the metre. In this example from Walt Whitman's 'Song of Myself', a comma interposes itself between the repeated vocative and the rest of the sentence, so that the verb can't exert its usual pulling power:

> See, steamers steaming through my poems,
> See, in my poems immigrants continually coming and landing,
> See, in arriere, the wigwam, the trail, the hunter's hut, the flat-
> boat, the maize-leaf, the claim, the rude fence, and the back-
> woods village,

Compare that with this unpunctuated passage by another great American, W.S. Merwin, in which line-breaks do the work of commas *and* full stops:

> then I saw that the flowers themselves
> were gone
> they were indeed gone
> I saw
> that my wife was gone
> then I saw that my daughter was gone
> afterward my eyes themselves were gone
> (from 'The Blind Seer of Ambon')

Whitman's comma before the 'and', often regarded as incorrect when used in a list, is known as an *Oxford comma*. Its role clearly has to do with register: it isn't demarking an entity, because the 'and' does that work. Nor is it 'closing the bracket' around a dependent clause. Instead, it widens the pause before the 'and', which gives that final phrase greater emphasis. Try reading this and similar sentences (Whitman is a past master of the long line) aloud, both with and without commas, to find how these act as stage directions.

Punctuation inserts pulse into metre in several ways. As well as working detail within a line – 'the wigwam, the trail, the hunter's hut, the flat-boat, the maize-leaf, the claim, the rude fence, and the backwoods village' – it is at its most evident when it *directs* cadence, especially through question and exclamation marks. Each entails a particular upward or downward music:

> Woe! I exclaimed – so it comes to this?
> Where are you, venerable ones, with your beards and wigs,
> Your nights spent by a candle, griefs of your wives?
> So a message saving the world is silenced forever?
> (Czeslaw Milosz, trans. Milosz and Robert Haas, 'Woe!')

Cadence, this rise and fall, is both entailed by and entails sense. It's striking how differently Merwin's and Whitman's sentences fall on the ear. Striking, too, is the way in which cadence can trump sense. One of the difficulties for emerging poets who regularly attend workshops or open mic sessions is that they can develop effective ways of reading that mask the shortcomings of a – perhaps unfinished – poem. This masking readily becomes habitual: so that not only does the poet fail to get the feedback which would help him to develop, but he comes to rely on that reading style as a marker of a good poem. Yet poems can arrive, like 'The March Calf' in Ted Hughes's poem, all knees and elbows. They are *not* necessarily beautifully cadenced – though think how hard it is to understand the music of a Les Murray poem unless you 'hear' the questioning Australian rise at the end of his lines. To write *for* cadence is to write with a kind of poetic false consciousness. It means you're writing for an experience of delivery and performance rather than for the intrinsic internal work of the poem itself.

On the other hand, cadence *can* serve as a useful indicator of possible difficulty. The 'dying fall' of the kind of phrase that doesn't follow through is irritating because it's the sign of a poem that may be indulging, or at least too-readily forgiving, itself. Repeated cadences suggest a poet who is stuck in her ways or who hasn't fully interrogated her ideas and images. A poem with the very same note at the end of every line, or even stanza, *fits too well* into the shape it has chosen for itself. It's being led by the music, rather than *making* music.

Used deliberately, on the other hand, cadence becomes a form of rhetoric. As you can hear in any famous political speech, it's a specific linguistic technique deployed in order to *add* to the work of language through a performative effect. This *is* allowing a text to be determined by its music: but it's conscious choice. It is also done for a reason *other than* the music itself: for emotional and semantic resonance.

Hardest to construct of all the workings of pulse is *scoring*: the rhythmic interplay of parts of a poem against themselves. Here, for example, is Shakespeare, using stepped lines of blank verse dialogue to score the way one speaker gives way to another:

Angus: We are sent
            To give thee, from our royal master, thanks;
            Only to herald thee into his sight,
            Not pay thee.
Ross: And, for an earnest of a greater honour,
            He bade me, from him, all thee Thane of Cawdor;
            In which addition, hail, most worthy Thane!
            For it is thine.
Banquo: What, can the devil speak true?
Macbeth: The Thane of Cawdor lives; why do you dress me
            In borrowed robes?
Angus: Who was Thane lives yet;
            But under heavy judgment bears that life . . .
                                             (*Macbeth*, Act 1, Scene 3)

And here is the contemporary Scottish poet John Burnside scoring the way one thought leads to another:

forgive me:
            I still can't resist
the sound of a fair in the distance
                        the new-crushed grass

those sixties songs
> the heat of the machines

>> ('Roads V')

Such spatial organization of a poem isn't decorative, but provides a record (a notation) of *how it sounds*.

This is also true of enjambment, where a phrase breaks across a line. One of the simplest examples is to be found in Edward Thomas's 'Adlestrop', whose first two stanzas in particular are a criss-cross of enjambment:

Yes. I remember Adlestrop—
The name, because one afternoon
Of heat the express-train drew up there
Unwontedly. It was late June.

The steam hissed. Someone cleared his throat.
No one left and no one came
On the bare platform. What I saw
Was Adlestrop—only the name

Here, the cadence of phrase and of line-break pull on each other, so that the micro-pause between the lines opens them out – that anticipation before the poet reveals what he saw – but also allows the key words 'came' and 'saw' to stand proud a little. An enjambment always adds to *sense*, whether by creating the feeling of how one thing leads to another (this is a travel poem, after all), or through stimulating speed or delay.

Examples like these underscore how powerful the *line* of poetry is as both an aural and a semantic unit. Generally speaking, short-lined verse will be brighter and more open in texture. On the other hand, one of the C.K. Williams's long-lined explorations gives a sense of capacity, both on the part of the exploring poet and within the hidden psychic material the work explores. Length solemnizes a poem, lending it a *sustained* music which suggests that it arises from sustained thinking.

As so often, the best guide here is speech pattern. The rhythms of actual talk never sound like those well-organized radio plays where one speech bears the almost-audible label 'Plot exposition' and another, 'Pointing out what the listener can't see'. As we *have* seen, what makes human speech predictable – what makes it seem to *fit* its own scoring – is the ear's native logic. In writing, therefore, it's essential to try each phrase aloud. Or 'aloud in the head', anyway: there's a difference between testing out how something sounds, whether or not you move your lips, and speed-reading 'for the page'. One of the ways to solve a poem when it gets stuck is to speak aloud the idea or image that comes next – without trying to make it 'sound like a poem'. It's a bit like explaining yourself to someone: maybe an imagined editor or translator. The rhythm of your speech has a natural momentum which can carry the poem past a difficulty.

To practise this, go back to listening to speech-rhythms, and this time try to lineate them. As we listen to speech – listen closely enough to transcribe it – we become able to predict likely rhythms as well as idiom. When his collection *A Book of Lives* was shortlisted for the 2007 T.S. Eliot Prize, Edwin Morgan, the Makkar or National Poet of Scotland, then eighty-seven, was too frail to attend the prize-giving ceremony. Instead, he was recorded by the Scottish Poetry Library, and that recording was played through the speakers of the Bloomsbury Theatre. Admittedly, this was poetry, not speech. But the amplification of Morgan's reading style – in short rushes, perhaps associated with shortness of breath – did two things. It showed the relationship between the poet's breath and the line of poetry and poetic thought; and it showed how the melodic line of Morgan's verse responds to something *beyond* the regular metre in which it happens to be written.

Transcribing speech allows us a similar amplification: especially if, in transcribing, we start a new line for each phrase. Something that is at least distantly related to a poem in free verse emerges from this process. That relationship exists because there's rhythmic and semantic *meaning* to the line-breaks. They aren't just arbitrary cut-ups in a block of prose, but record a *voice*: which, as we've seen, is the way a persona gets itself on to the page. Transcribing speech-rhythm also demonstrates how *musical* the human speaking voice is. It shows the importance of grammar – clause-making – in phrase-making, and hence the musicality of grammar itself. This music underlies free verse.

The best speech to transcribe in order to practise speech-rhythm lineation isn't dialogue but monologue. In workshops, I often ask members to work in pairs and take turns transcribing each other's account of some anecdote: anything from an old family story to what happened on the way to class. Such anecdotes work better than jokes or reminiscences because they're less likely to have acquired a set form of words, which may be rather ritualized and have lost some of the flexible music of speech. If you're working alone, you could try asking someone you know to tell you such an anecdote 'to help you with your writing'. You're not trying to trick them – though, at the same time, they don't need to know quite what you're using their words for. Or try to transcribe from the radio. When you read this speech back aloud, following its musical lines as you've recorded them, do you sound like the original speaker? Or have you tidied up their diction, trying to turn it from their kind of music into yours? Testing lineation in this way helps develop your ear. It can also provide you with a set of rhythmic forms or tropes to deploy alongside the heady rush of anapaest and dactyl and the dogmatic tramp of monosyllables.

Free verse must be exceptionally finely calibrated if it's to achieve musical coherence. There are many models, but no templates, for such poems. They require the poet to build them from the ground up. Though emerging writers are encouraged towards free verse, so that workshops won't be dominated by formal techniques, it is in fact among the hardest of forms to perfect. Balance and closure are especially important here. The sense of poetic necessity with which we greet the closing couplet of a sonnet, for example, is harder to discover in a new form. The solution we come up with has to work harder because the reader has never encountered *exactly* the same thing before.

In free verse, every poem works in a slightly different way – and every poet has a different relationship to the form. This relationship is primarily an individual sense of what such poetry can do. For example, women's writing is sometimes associated with a freer line than that of men's verse. 'Freer' doesn't mean, here, less disciplined, but having more of a sense of speeding forward, of flow or 'horizontal' connection. Even fairly demanding avant-garde poetry often seems, in the hands of women poets, to have more of an emotional line, a connectedness, than in the rugged hands of their male peers. This may be because of a conscious eschewal of 'the muscular' or 'the lapidary' as positive qualities to aim for; it may have to do with a kind of semi-conscious response to peer pressure, a kind of consensus; or it may arise at some entirely unconscious level from these writers' ways of being in the world. Whatever the reasons, as a phenomenon it's observable and therefore available as a model – to writers of *both* genders. For example, Jorie Graham's chopped-up lines seem to urge themselves onwards through their own gaps towards something the poem is working out. Anne Carson, especially in a book like *The Beauty of the Husband*, tangos her way across the page in long lines, stamping a cross-rhythm on to conventions of metre and diction. An interesting way to get some sense of gendered poetics is to browse any anthology of contemporary verse and guess the gender of authors of poems that particularly strike you.

Postmodern poetry is arguably at the furthest remove from formal metre. It deliberately resists the conventional, in register, sense and prosody, so that its readers can *hear afresh*. The Australian eco-poet John Kinsella sees poetry as part of his activism, and has written persuasively of the importance of *unexpected* line-breaks and diction, which ensure that the reader is never quite comfortable but instead has to read attentively. Kinsella argues that citizenship requires us to read actively and suspiciously, rather than near-passively. This is the reverse of the copy-writer's or politician's reliance on easy linguistic music, from tub-thumping crescendo to dying fall. Yet even here there are lyricists – largely though not exclusively women, such as Denise Riley and the late Veronica Forrest-Thomson – who create a melodic relationship between their images. The American John Ashbery is Post-modernism's foremost lyric poet.

All good poetry displays some tension, or sympathy, between the formal tropes it reworks and the individual 'voice' of the poet. It's just this *layering* of levels of *rhythmic music* that is one of the distinguishing features of good verse. In the next chapter we look at further layers of variation, as we examine creative disobedience.

6 Creative disobedience

Of Man's First Disobedience, and the Fruit
Of that Forbidden Tree . . .

John Milton, *Paradise Lost*

According to John Milton, and indeed the Bible, history starts
with a fruitful disobedience. Indeed, feminist theologians
have suggested that the whole story of the Fall – in which God
banishes the human couple from Paradise after the devil has
tempted Eve to eat from the Tree of Knowledge – shows us
how the creative and responsible principle of self-hood arises.
Individuation is achieved through knowledge: it could be a
parable of the way the infant separates from his mother
during the 'terrible twos'.

What has this got to do with writing? Well, the story of the
apple (or fig, as it was originally), is also a great founding
myth for poetry. A poem starts with creative disobedience: an
act of creative independence. Every new poem makes its own
version of an age-old theme or existing form. Independence
and its close neighbour, disobedience, are built in to the very
fabric of a poem.

But not everyone who writes poetry is consciously aware of
this. The all-too-familiar poem that is neither sparkling
pastiche nor literal translation, yet which nevertheless follows
a model so closely that it seems to lack an identity of its own,
is on the increase. The rise of apprentice-style workshops for

61

aspiring poets is an important development, one that allows access to disciplines and techniques that poets previously had to pick up ad hoc – or were lucky enough to receive through individual mentoring by personal contact, in traditionally privileged ways. Less happy, perhaps, is the formalization of that apprentice/master relationship in which two practitioners work alongside each other – one with a greater degree of expertise than the other, but both in, as it were, the same direction as each other – into a teacher–pupil power structure. When learning your *own* way of writing gets confused with the acquisition of expensive and life-changing qualifications, obedience to models and techniques that don't arise organically from your own development becomes a huge temptation. This is even more the case because Creative Writing tutors can, as teaching practice becomes the norm, turn into gatekeepers, exerting an additional, practical influence over new writers' careers. Anglo–American poetry – which comprises much of the poetry being written in English today – has for a while now been characterized by poets who earn their living as teachers, rather than as critics or editors. The result is that many of today's best-known poets rest their entire reputations on the shoulders of those they promote. That's not a situation conducive to fair critical reading; nor does it make it likely that *independent* new poets, however technically assured and well-read, are going to find much free space in which to develop.

Part of developing an authoritative poetic persona, and establishing your vision as a poet, is being prepared to obey your inner compass. It's really useful to check this regularly, even if you're already publishing books and winning prizes, in order to stop your work becoming complacent, self-referential – and dull. But for as long as it truly does point in a particular direction, whether that's syllabics or pentameter, narrative or confessional verse, it is important to listen to and take a bearing from your own sense of direction. Poetry composed 'from the outside in' may impress at first, through technical discipline, 'issue-relevance' or sheer fashionability, but it will be somehow lifeless, in a way every true reader can recognize. Fashionable poems are a bit like the pupil in class who wants to be picked by teacher: eager to show off how clever he is, he always gives the *expected* answer.

Yet these kinds of poems often win competitions for emerging poets, and I suspect that this is for two reasons. First, the obedient poem has become such a staple of the poetry scene that judges may not find anything out-of-the-ordinary about it – or, indeed, find any alternatives among the submissions. Second, such poems do better on a single read than they do in a book or magazine, where they can be returned to again and again. But what are they *for*? A poem that exists in order to lever its author into a particular position in the (tiny) world of poetry is not a poem in most recognized senses of the word. It certainly doesn't do the things we expect of poetry: refresh, transform, debate, ritualize. It's a poem-shaped emptiness held up against those expectations. And poets who can't move beyond this kind of writing won't develop.

Not all obedient poetry is written with cynicism, of course. Much of it just comes from humility. That's why the mantras of self-identification in this book's first chapter, however awkward they are, matter. It's 'poetic authority' that gives us the freedom to build a true poem, one that is its own version of itself. Disobedience is a symptom of confidence, of having found an independent way of going on. A poem that is overworked can still become obedient, as can a poem with no necessity of its own. Interestingly and paradoxically – since one might expect that there would be nothing left to say about the 'Great Things': death, suffering, love, the problem of spiritual or religious meaning – it's generally occasional poems, arising from the most arbitrary of starting-points (for example, in workshops), which have a tendency to resemble one another. They're more likely to be just going through the motions, without desire or excitement.

That desire and excitement has to be located in your poem rather than in your original experience. Whether or not something really happened, and triggered strong emotions, is no proof that those emotions are *in the poem*. If this sounds contradictory – a bit like saying that poems suffer whether they're written with or without a strong initial impulse – it's not. Having the impulse *towards a poem* isn't the same as having any old emotional impulse. It's emotionally much closer to whatever feeling the poem ends up describing than whatever's happened 'in real life'. Here's Amy Clampitt writing about the impulse towards a poem: 'Thank you for liking "Venice Revisited". It was rewritten several times – but ending upon the moon came as a total surprise as I wrote it' (17 September 1984). And here is Elizabeth Bishop: 'And here I must confess (and I imagine most of our contemporaries would confess the same thing) that I am green with envy of your kind of assurance. I feel that I could write in as much details about my Uncle Artie, say, – but what would be the significance? Nothing at all. . . . Whereas all you have to do is put down the names!' (14 December 1957).

Both these great American poets can characterize the impulse that starts a poem with such informality because each assumes she's writing to someone (Clampitt to the critic Helen Vendler; Bishop to the poet Robert Lowell) who recognizes what they mean. They don't imagine we're listening over their shoulder. This *easy denotation* is a sign of something shared. And something similar characterizes the light, organic touch of a poem that is more than simply obedient. It's able to characterize, rather than labour to describe. Its writer *knows* – since she's writing from life – that she's noting something shared. This is as true of the physical world of the senses as it is of the inner life. Here, for example, is Bishop on Cabo Frio, in Brazil, to the editor Katharine White: 'I read . . . under a beach umbrella on a lonely little beach with not another soul on it – a beach that is almost like a segment of the Maine coast, except that the water is warm and the cacti were all in bloom – rocks, islands, a turtle swimming around and raising his head every once in a while, even a small waterfall' (15 January 1963). Or here is Clampitt writing, again to Vendler, from London: 'We go to Stratford this weekend; I've never been there, idiotic as it may sound, but that idiocy must go on no longer' (4 May 1983).

John Keats's famous portrait of spontaneity, 'Ode to a Skylark', who 'Pourest thy full heart / In profuse strains of unpremeditated art', is also an – albeit idealized – representation of his own poetic practice. The hard-working boy wonder, both doctor and emerging poet, lover and invalid, must have needed a philosophy of what we now call time-poverty. For him, that was Romanticism and the idea of poetry as unpredictable, *sui generis*, and arising independently of effort and concentration. Perhaps this was how he coped with the frustrations of poverty and illness. Some of this early Romanticism became systematized, especially by Samuel Taylor Coleridge, into a celebration of, and fascination with, dream-imagery. Coleridge's use of opiates is not unconnected to this imaginative disobedience, and it's perhaps no surprise that he explored narrative fantasy in *The Rime of the Ancient Mariner* and 'Kubla Khan'. But just as important is his need to believe in 'a person from Porlock' who interrupted the compositional flow of 'Kubla Khan' – and with it a *spontaneous* initial creativity. That authentic 'first fine careless rapture', as Robert Browning wrote about another kind of song (in 'Home Thoughts from Abroad'), was for the Romantics – and has remained to this day among emergent poets – a kind of article of faith. To some extent this is good, to some extent bad, faith. Spontaneity of impulse isn't quite the same as spontaneity of composition: it's certainly not the same as throwing down an unworked set of lines and thinking that's a finished poem. But it does remind us that there may be things we *want* to write, and that belong to the independent, personal realm.

So how – apart from becoming aware of the impulse towards a poem – do you *practise* avoiding obedience? Isn't that another paradox? Well, it is possible. Breaking your own internal laws, the ones that are so habitual they're 'below the radar', is great practice for good writing. It's all about resisting the lure of the comfort zone. When my friend Jean started to feel stale at work, she began crossing the road in a slightly different place every day in order not to become truly stuck in a rut. And there are lots of other small disobediences that can add spice to your daily life:

- Always choose a different chair – in the café, in meetings, in the dentist's waiting room.
- Buy a different newspaper one day this week.
- Ask to borrow some small item of clothing from someone you know well – maybe a scarf or a pair of socks – for a few hours.
- Don't use your usual salad dressing or condiments.
- Smile at a stranger.

The list is easy to add to. And you're not trying to live in Keatsian doubts and uncertainties, putting *everything* you rely on in question – it's just a chance to have some fun . . .

Once you've tried out the gentle art of disobedience, it's time to bring it into your writing. Take two or three poems you like and admire – contemporary examples are probably slightly easier to use here – and challenge yourself to change just one word in each. It needs to be a change that makes sense, of course: challenge yourself to make an improvement. But it could also add to or change the poem's existing meaning.

Now read a poem of your own, one you wrote a little while ago. Set yourself the task of changing just one word, in the same way. You're out of the rut of the poem and so you have a chance to refresh it – and yourself. This can feel oddly liberating. Perhaps it's because it means thinking without *oughts*. You've no further responsibility to any of the poems you're playing with, whether they're by you or someone else. Disobedience, after all, is a shoe-horn into a different you: into a new imaginative world full of unknown and unpredictable things.

7 The power of five: writing from the senses

1874, July 12 – I noticed the smell of the big cedar, not just in passing it but always at a patch of sunlight on the walk a little way off. I found the bark smelt in the sun and not in the shade and I fancied too this held even of the smell it shed in the air.

Gerard Manley Hopkins, *Journal*

I once read a review in which a poem about hearing was criticized for not being about the world of the senses! This was at a point, at the start of the millennium, when a fashion for the visual still had a stranglehold on British poetry. The funnelling of attention on to a handful of poets of one generation, through a promotion based on *Granta's* 'Best of Young British Novelists' model, meant poetic authority was concentrated in the hands of a few poets and their publishers, and orthodoxies were everywhere.

The baby-boomer poets were passionately opposed to abstract thought. They followed a poetic generation who'd been partly nurtured by Louis MacNeice, Anthony Thwaite and George MacBeth at the BBC; who were largely university-educated; who sometimes worked as critics – and whom these younger poets saw as fusty. The baby-boomers were in love with surfaces. They believed in the evidence of their own eyes. They wanted specifics of place and narrative. They did *not* want writing to fall in love with itself and get carried away. It was as if a happy snapper had displaced an *auteur*; or someone were peering in disgust at a Bergman clip and complaining that it 'just isn't life-like'. Under this poetic convention – William Carlos Williams's 'No ideas but in things' – there were no inner resonances, just outer activity. An 'inner life' was seen as a contradiction in terms. So it became the orthodoxy that writing must be rooted in the concrete world: or at least in *observing* it. Poetry didn't suddenly become literally three-dimensional, of course: that had to wait for the meta-texts of the digital age. Concrete poetry – mapping shapes with the arrangements of words – may have been a hit in primary schools, but it wasn't widely used in published work, as it had been in the 1960s. As in all orthodoxies, inconsistencies went unquestioned.

'Observation' was increasingly narrowed down to mean *visual* observation. This was the age of the screen, and of rapidly developing visual fluency. It was an era of 'computer graphics' – in everything from educational displays and games to desk-top publishing – and of videos for everything, including commercial music. That visual culture hasn't gone away. We live alongside it with a high degree of familiarity. But we remain embodied humans, and the concrete world is more than merely visible – it's audible and tactile, it smells and tastes. Indeed, the sensations that are *closest* to us – whether pain or desire – are the least visual.

So a review which complained that a poem wasn't about the world of the senses because it was about *hearing* instead of *looking* was simply an example of thinking prevalent at the time. And it remains something we need to struggle against as writers. Even the word we use for simile, symbol, illustration or metaphor alike – *image* – suggests the visual. An *imago* is, literally, a *visual* representation. In fact, we're *always* using the term metaphorically when we apply it to descriptions of the material world, even when they're descriptions of what that world *looks* like, because words, unlike visual media, can't *reproduce* something visible but only record it. Language isn't a view, but a signpost: not a photograph, but a map.

'Not a photograph, but a map': language also has the power to reveal *more* than we'd get from looking at the original. It's not merely the poet's observation, but their *understanding*, of the physical world that makes the concrete detail in a poem worth having. That's how it adds to the sum of things. Just as a map tells us about things which we can see – the relative heights of mountains, or the ultimate source of a river – so a poem's 'images' may be something different from, but aren't less than, the world they borrow from.

This additionality – think 'added value!' – is also what powers the practice of *ekphrasis*, one of the most sense-specific of genres. Ekphrasis is the representation of a work of art in one medium by another. Mussorgsky's *Pictures at an Exhibition* is a famous example of visual-musical ekphrasis. The music evokes a posthumous exhibition, held in St Petersburg in 1874, of the painter Viktor Hartmann's work. Representations of specific paintings are linked by the famous promenade theme, as the spectator tours the virtual gallery.

It's a form of genre translation. Illustration and stage-and-costume design could almost be seen as ekphrastic. But they *accompany* the original, in the same way that choreography does its score, rather than having to *stand in* for it. Film adaptations of books aren't generally ekphrastic either: they can't represent the texture and indeed *textuality* of the original writing. They simply re-tell the story. However, there is a real body of ekphrastic poetry that attempts to capture visual art. Famous examples include Robert Browning's 'My Last Duchess', whose eponymous portrait is entirely fictional, and 'At the Musée des Beaux Arts' by W.H. Auden, about an actual painting by Brueghel. Auden's poem has itself become an object of transformation: a poem by Siriol Troup elides what the original has to say with a famous photo of Auden and his lover Chester Kallman at a pavement café in Venice. This is a good example of how ekphrasis, like a description of the concrete world, requires the poet to *add* something. Another is the long title-sequence of David Harsent's

Marriage, which celebrates the female nude, as well as seeing relationship as a process of contemplation, through Pierre Bonnard's repeated paintings of his wife Marthe de Meligny. Such ekphrastic transformations remind us that poetry is never a camera. It can't simply *reproduce* the sensory world, but *turns* it into its own material.

The best way to experience this transformative action – as well as how ekphrasis is sense-specific – is to write an ekphrastic poem yourself. It's easier to write about an image than about music, which is usually abstract and therefore harder to articulate: and easier to write about a painting or print than about a photograph, where the medium itself can disappear into the image. So I suggest you pick a picture you know well. Start by making notes of everything you *notice* about the image: the texture of the paint, the way the colours make your eyes swim, as well as what the picture tells you. Now note down what you think it's *making* of its subject: is it pejorative? Is it sexist? Is it borrowing religious iconography? And, if so, how does that change the resonance of the picture? Finally, look at how it *organizes* that representation: is there a single mass of colour that dominates? Or, as with Auden's Brueghel, is the foreground really the background to the main story? Remember, what you're evoking is the *picture-ness* of this picture, not just its subject matter. Once you've thought about it in each of these ways, you have the raw material for ekphrasis. But to transform the notes into an ekphrastic poem, you still need additionality. You need a *reason* to re-present the picture as a poem. What do words offer that the original medium didn't? What will turn the picture into a poem, not just a catalogue description in verse? What moves you about it? When did you first notice it and what did it mean to you then? How does it speak to your own experience, whether great or small (of being caught in a rainstorm – or of breaking up with someone you loved greatly)? The *meaning* you bring to the poem is what breathes the ekphrastic transformation into it.

Incidentally, this chapter is proceeding as if you the reader could not possibly have a sensory impairment. This is just shorthand for starting every sentence with 'Providing you can do so. . .'. If you *do* have such an impairment, however slight, I hope you'll read according to your own experience. Embodied experience is exactly what it's about, after all. That there have been many fine poets, from Homer and John Milton to Jack Clemo, with visual as well as auditory impairment simply proves the point. Poetry is not a screen on to which a purely visual world is projected, at a safe distance from three-dimensional embodiment. After all, the old idea of the blind seer – whether they be Tiresias, Samson in Gaza, or a blindfolded Justice – is based on the idea that profound, impartial observations are made by those who see beyond the 'look' of things.

For poets who are distracted by their visual sense, though, sound can be particularly helpful in learning not to take a purely visual account of the world on trust. This is because the aural, like the visual, it is a *continuous, joined-up stream of information*. My collie Juno steers round the world at least in part by smell. That's what *interests* her; and, if she were a poet, it would be the sense that would dominate her work because it's how she receives meaningful information – about other dogs, food, and whether she's been somewhere before. But, even with her superior canine olfactory equipment, there are long gaps where Juno is receiving virtually no such information. She's simply waiting for the next stimulus. Much the same applies, for us, to taste and touch. Though I'm sitting at my laptop to type this, and can feel the percussion of the keyboard through my fingertips, the warmth of the sun, and the slight friction of the chair on my backbone, my senses of touch and taste are not as alive as they will be later today, when I take the train to London in time for supper with my partner. Sound and sight, though, are continually in play. I can hear a small plane droning overhead – I recognize the engine-note and so I know that a glider is being hauled up the thermals of this fine blue sky, which has got the birds singing their spring calls, even though it's only February. Next-door's chickens are chirruping and clucking and, again, I know without reflection that this means they're laying well. I can hear the bird-scarer guns over towards the river – the spring wheat is up – and something alights on the flat roof of the shed, sounding heavy enough to be the thrush I heard sing earlier. A pigeon goes winging off; so, higher up, is a transatlantic jumbo on its way west. All the while, I'm generating the muted patter of my laptop keyboard.

For the hearing writer, such a suite of sounds accompanies every moment of writing. It's worth taking the time to list them accurately: this is ideal practice for sensory observation and also a useful shift in habits. Writing always benefits from getting yourself to think slightly differently, even if it's just a temporary shift of attention. It's good to do this exercise with each sense, and periodically. As you list, try to *characterize* each sound or sensation. What are its qualities – of texture and volume? When does it occur? What does it remind you of? This exercise is a reminder of the resources available to us. It allows you to develop what may be little-used parts of your sensory palette.

But it's also worthwhile going further into the world of sound, which is important for both the content and the form of poetry. We take it for granted that poetry and sound are intimately related. After all, the idea of the *lyric* is musical but also has to do with a peculiarly poetic 'feel' or sensibility. The term comes from rhetoric; an approach to writing that identifies thoughts with their forms, the sound *with* its fury.

That's a useful reminder of what the form of poetry is *for*. And all poetics concern themselves, to a large extent, with the *organization* of sound in rhyme, metre, assonance and so on. But *making* sound isn't the same as *listening*, as anyone who has ever been in an argument knows. I believe good writing also pays attention to the sounds around us. Among the many well-known poems about specifically musical experience, Tomas Tranströmer's 'Allegro', which opens 'After a black day, I play Haydn, / and feel a little warmth in my hands', is part of the wider ekphrastic tradition. So is D.H. Lawrence's

'Piano', in which the narrator is a listener rather than a performer:

Softly, in the dusk, a woman is singing to me;
Taking me back down the vista of years, till I see
A child sitting under the piano, in the boom of the tingling
          strings
And pressing the small, poised feet of a mother who smiles as
          she sings.

In spite of myself, the insidious mastery of song
Betrays me back, till the heart of me weeps to belong
To the old Sunday evenings at home, with winter outside
And hymns in the cosy parlour, the tinkling piano our guide.

So now it is vain for the singer to burst into clamour
With the great black piano appassionato. The glamour
Of childish days is upon me, my manhood is cast
Down in the flood of remembrance, I weep like a child for the
          past.

Poems like these allow us to glimpse the very *process* of listening to the music. Often, that experience is recorded – as it is by Lawrence – as a chance to let the mind wander. The famous passage in E.M. Forster's *Howard's End*, where Helen Schlegel hears Beethoven in a concert and tries to 'make sense of' it, shows us her partial inability to concentrate, or at least to follow the music, and converts musical form into a metaphor:

For the Andante had begun – very beautiful, but bearing a family likeness to all the other beautiful Andantes that Beethoven had written, and, to Helen's mind, rather disconnecting the heroes and shipwrecks of the first movement from the heroes and goblins of the third. She heard the tune through once, and then her attention wandered, and she gazed at the audience, or the organ, or the architecture.

73

However, some 'musical' poems, such as T.S. Eliot's *Four Quartets*, based on late chamber music of Ludwig van Beethoven, or the 'Four Quartets' in John Burnside's book *Gift Songs* (2006), take the opposite approach. They refer to the movement of thought *within the music* which is their model, rather than to an experience of *musicality*. In this they actually come closer to *listening* than simple ekphrasis does. The music is simply a vehicle through which ideas the poem shares were first conveyed. These poems listen *through* the music to what it expresses.

Behind all these 'musical' transcriptions lurks the deeper idea that *every* poem is a kind of transcription or translation, into poetic form, of the world of thought or experience. In other words, poetic attention is John Keats's wide-open 'negative capability'. Virginia Woolf's wonderful 'If I could catch the feeling I would: the feeling of the singing of the real world . . .' expresses the same idea. Gwyneth Lewis alludes to the darker side of this kind of closeness when she says that 'poetry is a form of energy that links the electricity of your truth to the world around you. Abusing the process, which links deeply with the subconscious, is likely to cause an artist big psychological problems.'

Listening is a hot-line to poetic attention. At a time of emerging ecological awareness, where we're *placed* – in the three-dimensional, all-too-concrete world – turns out to be existentially important. But at the same time we do live in the era of the screen. Ours is a highly developed visual, and virtual, culture. Yet if we confine our attention to the visual, we actually distance ourselves from the world of experience. Sight, unlike smell, taste or touch, holds the world at a distance. The child lying in long grass and squinting between its blades knows that things can become *too close to see*. On the other hand, sound is rather like touch, taste and smell. We experience it as continuous with the body. Whether you dive under water that bubbles in your ears, or hear a wasp buzz, but can't work out 'where the sound is coming from', you know that the locus of that hearing is 'in your own head'. These 'other' four senses, the ones beyond vision, bring experience close to your own body. This means that they are the senses which, in the text, *give a body* to the narrator and the reader.

That's particularly noticeable when a poem adopts the sound-world of its subject. We're used to onomatopoeia, where the sound of a word reproduces the sound of what it names. An extension of this is using the sounds of words to evoke the mood they describe. Plosives such as *t* and *p* may convey anger or quick-thinking; a softened *s* and *th*, as well as the more muted vowels (*u* and *e*), may indicate tenderness. One of the ways in which both Eliot and Burnside evoke the long, demanding lines of great quartet music is by using slurs of breath, or *rubatos*, which break – in Burnside's case – across stepped lines. So there are several ways of paying attention in sound, as well as an infinite variety of sounds to pay attention to in the world around us. This means that listening is a way of paying attention that notices complexity as well as imme-diacy. When it brings that experience into a poem, it can show us something about the complexity of experience in general.

Concentrating on sound, then, can be a great way into poem-making, and the rest of this chapter is taken up with an exercise in writing poetry which starts with that sense. It's an approach that is primarily concerned with the start, rather than the end, of writing a poem; because working like this offers the opportunity to break open any formal, 'musical' habits you already have and to bring in something new.

First, go back to listening. Identify four sounds you can hear right now and note down the *pattern* each makes. For instance, wind may seem to blow in long phrases, or kids' shouts to cluster. If you're indoors with the windows shut, notice the ticking of electrical appliances, or your own pulse. As you choose each sound, note the rhythmic *variety* by which you're surrounded.

Now select one sound or group of sounds and, still in note form, describe it more fully, moving out into metaphor – and breaking as many rules as you can. Use mixed metaphor, synaesthesia, mimicry and macaronic. Move in, and then out, of personification. Ask yourself (and note down) why you were drawn to *that* sound. What are its *resonances* for you? This builds up relationships of meaning, just as you did with the ekphrastic poem.

You've done all this in note form so that your usual poetic 'voice' won't break in and take over. If it does, your ear will fall back into its usual behaviour. Now, to allow your diction the chance to take on new, unfamiliar rhythms, pay especial attention to human speech rhythms. Go back to the notebook you used in Chapter 3, and look through it until you pick up your transcriptions of just one speaker. Notice where their speech lends itself to lineation through pause, stress and repetition. Try to reconstruct a sense of their own individual music in pulse and phrasing. These are the kinds of sound-shapes you hear in a hotel or through a house-wall, and which childhood hears as it falls asleep. Elizabeth Bishop evokes them part-way through 'The Moose':

> A dreamy divigation
> begins in the night,
> a gentle, auditory,
> slow hallucination . . .
>
> In the creakings and noises,
> An old conversation
> – not concerning us,
> but recognizable, somewhere,
> back in the bus:
> Grandparents' voices
>
> uninterruptedly
> talking, in Eternity:
> . . .

Return to your new notes on sounds. 'Listen to' (concentrate on) your memory of what it was like listening to the sound in the first place. Now, using a diction – in particular, a rhythm – appropriate for that sound, write about the moment of that *experience*. Short, staccato lines might suit trampling footsteps, or birdsong; lengthy, expansive lines might evoke a plane passing overhead. But this moment of experience may require you to include all sorts of emotional or narrative material, as well as that of other senses – even sight! Nevertheless, your poem has been *led* by the experience of listening.

Rhythmically sophisticated diction doesn't have to be *mimetic*. It can be evocative, too. Emily Dickinson's dashes, like Jorie Graham's more than a hundred years later, don't mimic the literal breathlessness of a physical effort but evoke the psychological effort of prayer and thought. The 'Anglican' line-breaks of R.S. Thomas's later verse, where a significant word doesn't end a line but starts the next, echo the conventions of *The Book of Common Prayer* and give his work a liturgical character, even at its most intimately confessional. This exercise should allow you to break out into some of the possibilities sound offers, not least by letting you escape from old habits. When you polish the poem in your own usual way, you'll find yourself coming up against the unexpected in your own writing. You may feel that you've produced a piece that is transitional: that it listens towards a new music but hasn't yet fully shaken off how you normally write. Don't be afraid of such transitions. They do *not* mean you can only write successfully in the ways you always have. Quite the reverse: such a poem illustrates how you can engage with new ways of writing. The more frustrated you feel, the more you wish it were closer to a new music, the closer you are to making that happen.

8 Sympathetic magic: metaphor and simile

Eye of newt, and toe of frog
Wool of bat, and tongue of dog
William Shakespeare, *Macbeth*, Act 4, Scene 1

Some of the earliest poems in the English tradition are Anglo-Saxon charms. They aren't part of the literate, Latin tradition, but a kind of folk poetry:

Wenne, wenne,   wenchichenne,
her ne scealt þu timbrien,   ne nenne tun habben . . .

O wen, wen   little [chicken] wen,
Here you shall not build   not have your abode,
But you must go north   to that nearby hill
For there, wretched one,   is a brother.

If this is just medicine, why bother with poetic form? The answer is, of course, that poetry's heightened diction seems appropriate for the important occasions that require magic – such as healing. And, perhaps, because a degree of mystification is necessary if the person casting the spell is to be believed. It's in this sense of *occasion*, as much as in catharsis, that the origins of ritual and liturgy lie.

Charms like this exist in most languages, often collected by

78

ethnographers though increasingly relished by poets. For example, Romanian literary language was standardized, in part by national poet Mihau Eminsecu, in the late nineteenth century, when the nation state we know today emerged. But Romanian, a Latin language in a sea of Slav tongues (not to mention Hungarian), had been *spoken* in the region for centuries. It's the language of charms like this one, collected by the poet Ioana Ieronim:

Ninety-nine serpents –
ninety-nine flaming beasts –
go to Ion
Slip in by his shirt-collar
squat in his heart
scald him burn him
turn his eyes to my eyes
his face to my face
his path to my house
Make him see me in the distance
a fine-feathered peacock
make him pick me out as basil among weeds
make him tease me among the girls
Like following gold and silver
fall in step with my words
with my walk
with my dance

These charms are relished by poets because of their apparent cousin-ship to poetry. As well as a heightened diction, they employ sympathetic magic. That's to say, they use something that is *like* or *a part of* a problem in order to refer to and deal with the thing itself. In the literary context, of course, this is called description, or simile. But here it's still a linguistic version of sympathetic magic, which brings a similar *object* to bear on the person or illness the charm acts upon. We can particularly imagine this linguistic magic being used when, as in the Anglo-Saxon example the sympathetic object is *larger* and *less* convenient than the original. The tumulus it resembles is a lot more unwieldy than a 'wen' or wart! The Romanian text given implies that ninety-nine – what? Twigs? Grass-blades? Hairs? – are *transformed* by incantation into the 'serpents . . . flaming beasts' the girl needs.

Each *representation* has the same powers as whatever it stands-in for. In other words, here, *naming* has the same powers as what it names. This is just how poetic metaphor works. It was Julia Kristeva who first made the distinction between a symbol and a sign. She points out that a symbol – such as the relic of a saint, or their statue, in medieval Europe – is full of the power of the original. Touch the toe of the statue, or glimpse the bones of the saint, and they will heal you just as the saint would in person. But the 'Death of God' in the twentieth-century West has meant the degradation of a symbol into a sign: something that merely indicates what's beyond itself, like a signpost or a map.

From a poet's point of view, a simile works like a sign. It points to something other than itself, and maintains a parallel existence with that original. As with parallel lines, the two sides of a simile never meet. In a simile, the wart would simply be *like* a tumulus. It could not 'turn into' it. Similes provide observations, equally useful in describing either a patient's skin or the Saxon landscape. 'Like' yokes the two sides of a simile together – and keeps them apart. A *simile* is built on *similarity*. Resemblance is something apparent rather than actual. In a metaphor, on the other hand, what's brought in *stands in for* the original. As the original Greek tells us, in *meta-phor* something is *carried across* from one place to another. Once the wart *is* an earthwork, it can be far away on a distant hillside. Once the Romanian's little bundle has turned into flaming serpents, it's able to harry the beloved. The metaphor performs sympathetic magic.

No wonder that it seems stronger than simile. The metaphor seems to need to be *earned*, by either context or register. It also requires stronger assent, a suspension of critical belief, in order to carry out its magic. To accept a metaphor, and not say 'That makes no sense!' means having to carry yourself across into it.

Here are some astonishing, unlikely metaphors:

> The night became tranquil and complete, I woke up
> as a flower and breathed by the garden fence.
> (Mahmoud Darwish, trans. Fady Joudah, 'Tuesday and the
> Weather is Clear')

And:

> I watch for her until she's really there,
> crossing open fields strewn with limbs
> she has to pick her way through very carefully
> in order to get safely home to me
> (Selima Hill, 'My Sister's Tooth')

And:

> Sorrow rises and falls, comes near with its deep spoons
> (Pablo Neruda, trans. Stephen Tapscott, 'Love Sonnets LV')

Yet each works according to its own poetic logic. The Darwish is part of a dream-like, incantatory poem exploring how to *be*; Hill's poem is part of a strongly felt book about the family as, in this case literally, 'a minefield'; Neruda's love poem has a personal domestic resonance, but also a national political one, as befitted his very public poetic role.

We need to pause here to think about naming. Like the Homeric *Iliad*, early Nordic and Anglo-Saxon verse employed kennings, compound terms that could describe or name key characters or places, just like proper names. Here, for example, Beowulf attracts two in as many lines:

> brego Beorht-Dena   biddan wille,
> eodor Scyldinga,   anre bene:
> (*Beowulf*, lines 428–9)

81

In Seamus Heaney's translation:

> And so, my request, O king of Bright-Danes.
> Dear prince of the Shieldings . . .

Kennings didn't only help the metre along: their use was incantatory. *Ascribing* qualities can leave them as supplementary, but *naming* someone as their possessor makes those qualities a matter of identity. It brings them across to stand *in the place of* the person you ascribe them to. Such symbol-formation works in the same way as a metaphor. For example, call someone a liar and some of the mud sticks. Hear someone being addressed as Archbishop and you see them differently. Call a chair uncomfortable and whoever sits in it will wonder whether they're comfortable. Identifying things in a certain way changes the powers those things and people actually have. Small wonder that poets sometimes like to see themselves as shamans, summoning up whatever they wish or, like Australian aboriginal peoples, singing their world into being.

Of course, it's possible to test the potential of metaphor without worrying about magical or spiritual practices. One way to do so is by looking at emotion. Finding metaphors for strong feelings, including unhappy ones, means finding an *equal register* as well as an *apt* sensory image. Suicidal depression is *not* simply dreary like a rainy day in Milton Keynes, though it might be as powerful as the Niagara Falls. But is depression watery at all? Or is it something altogether more steely and unbending?

Part of the brilliance of Sylvia Plath is that she understood the stakes involved in metaphor in her late great poems *about* furious despair, such as 'Lady Lazarus':

> A sort of walking miracle, my skin
> Bright as a Nazi lampshade,
> My right foot

A paperweight,
My face a featureless, fine
Jew linen.

Peel off the napkin

. . .

Plath's writing shows us something about the way metaphor is *realized*. Though it can simply name an attribute or object, when a metaphor is more fully explored and inhabited it becomes *more potent*. After all, this is a symbol, there to take the place of its object: it's not the fleeting allusion of a sign. A good exercise at this point, then, is to turn a strong emotion into metaphor. Chose one you're familiar with, even if it seems banal or negative – resentment, envy – rather than something possibly more heroic or dignified that you'd have to guess at. And, if this exercise is at all likely to take you into difficult emotional territory, make sure you've someone you can turn to for support.

First, think about the *texture* of the emotional experience you've picked. Is it a long sweep, low-down and creeping, or sharply painful? Second, think about *register*: the kind of intensity you want your metaphor to have. Of course, you want it to be clear as a bell, but you don't want to sound over-the-top (if you describe the boredom of standing in a queue in terms of torture) or, worse still, bathetic (if you describe protracted torture of a political prisoner in terms of queuing at the Post Office). Register is to some degree the *point* of what metaphor has to say. For a metaphor *chooses the stakes* for what you're talking about, making something grand or trivial, glamorous or quotidian, as well as showing the reader what you want them to feel. Register is your generator of readerly emotion (*affect*).

Third, think about how *familiar* or unlikely you'd like the metaphor to be. You need it to be fresh, so that it doesn't fall flat like cliché, but you don't want to be so wacky that the reader has no notion what you're talking about. The very best image-makers have a great ability to synthesize – to free-associate and let themselves be *reminded* of other things in a given context – rather than being purely inventive. *Pure* invention leads to surrealism, the original play between distantly related images. This is a wonderful genre – but it's not metaphorical. A famous surrealist image, for example in the work of great yet often-forgotten English-language surrealists like David Gascoyne or Leonora Carrington, isn't a metaphor for something else. Instead, it's a dream-like set of juxtapositions, which the mind can play with precisely because it's up to each of us to choose the links those juxtapositions suggest.

Hooks of affinity run between a metaphor and its original. These affinities are: resemblance (the metaphor *fits*), appropriateness (the metaphor *suits*) and affect (the metaphor *moves* the reader in a way that the original means to). The original – the pity of war, a beautiful woman – *may* move the reader, but it may require a metaphor precisely because it *doesn't* readily engage us. The homesickness of an adult sleeping rough, for example, is traditionally seen as less sympathetic than that of a child orphan. Metaphor can carry the reader over to another way of seeing such things. Small wonder it's in the grammar of political rhetoric.

As you find metaphors for your emotional experiences, be aware that one of the things you're trying to do is to persuade the reader of your own emotional reality. You're trying to 'make it come alive' for them. Implicitly, as with all writing, you want them to agree with you. We'll look at this in more detail in Chapter 16, when we encounter the Ideal Reader.

Many political clichés are metaphors. For example, 'I believe in America' employs a powerful suggestion of faith, especially significant for a culture with strong religious traditions, to characterize the speaker's investment in that socio-political fact. It 'spiritualizes' the candidate's quest for power. Other political metaphors work through synecdoche or metonym: the part stands in for the whole. The queen who visits injured soldiers in a field hospital is indicating that her concern extends to *all* soldiers injured in the line of duty. The president who kisses a baby is kissing not just that baby, but *the idea of the nation's babies* – and, by extension (metaphor within a metaphor), its future identity. The baby also represents a country's vulnerable citizens, hence the president is embracing the idea of collective responsibility.

In one of the most famous literary examples of synecdoche, sails stand in for the Athenian fleet. This is interestingly empirical: at a distance the sails of a tall ship are all that one can see, and early audiences would have been quite accustomed to seeing sails on the horizon and *knowing that this meant* there was a fleet of ships attached to them. Tracing the concrete roots of metonym in this way is a useful technique for making it watertight. As well as obeying the three general rules of metaphor, metonym has to be tested for the necessity of *that* part standing in for the whole. A fin stands in for a shark; a nib for a pen; a nose, in the work of a cartoonist, for a face. A shaft cannot stand in for a pen. It's too unspecific: is it the handle of a garden spade or a giant industrial chimney? Unlike an eye or a mouth, a nose is distinctively *human*. The shark's fin borrows all sorts of resonance from popular culture, from the film *Jaws* to cartoons of desert islands with circling fins – and it does so because, as with the ships' sails, it derives from actual experience: this really is the way we encounter sharks.

If metaphor brings information together, simile makes explicit the distance within a comparison. The respectful space between the two sides of a simile is maintained in a number of ways which are, in effect, rules governing *the grammar of comparison*. Although they apply to metaphor too, they're more fully incorporated there. Similes, on the other hand, are one of the few rhetorical tropes to show their workings – like a Richard Rogers building whose pipe-work is all on the outside.

First, the two sides of a simile can't come from the same category as each other, or else nothing new is understood. You've simply made a comparison. For example, to say the song of a robin is as sweet as that of a thrush is not a simile but a comparison. We are still thinking of the robin's call as bird-song. But to say it's as sweet as a sherbet lemon *is* a simile, because the comparison has stepped out of category.

On the other hand, it's not a very successful simile. There's a sharpness to a sherbet lemon that the robin's song doesn't have. Things that *could* be characterized as piercingly sweet but with a sour edge, like a sherbet lemon, might include a nostalgic reminiscence, or someone singing sweetly but off-key. So rule number two needs to be precise not only about which aspect of something is being compared – but what the characteristics of that aspect are. Under-thought similes, including clichés, simply don't work because they don't ring true. In the case of a clichéd simile, this may be because it's too one-size-fits-all: 'She was like a breath of fresh air' might mean either 'she was rather a shock to the system' or 'she lifted one's spirits, one had a sense of freedom'. Or it might simply mean 'she did things in a new way' – for good or ill. Such lack of precision gets carried over into clichés so familiar that we no longer even hear the simile in them. 'She felt as if her heart were breaking' is actually not a bad description of the physical sensations of pressure and strain in the chest when you're struggling with profound and sudden grief. But it sheds no new light. In fact, you could say that a cliché is a phrase or trope from which the light has gone out (which is itself a metaphor).

The third pitfall of the simile is the kind that simply isn't true whether or not it's new: though this problem is particu-larly acute with clichés, because we no longer hear what they're actually saying. The false simile sits on experience like a dustsheet does on furniture, blurring and transforming the outlines. An example is: 'child-like innocence'. What blurs this description is our *own* experience of having been children. We all *know* that children are not innocent, except sexually; it's just that the reach of their crimes is so much smaller than an adult's.

So a simile needs precision. Even once you've identified the characteristic you're focusing on, you need to find an accurate match for it. British writers often teach this, in workshops, through the Furniture Game. That's a short title (actually a metonym itself) for a sort of anti-riddle. In this 'game', everyone takes turns to describe themselves in similes. The usual construction is 'If I were a [category], I'd be a . . .' The game takes its title from what's often the first category: 'If I were a piece of furniture, I'd be a . . .' The idea is not to give your favourite example of each, but to pick something you feel describes you. So you might *want* to be, or to own, a regency chaise longue. But you might *feel* more like the kitchen stool that gets sat on and kicked about and used as a stepladder, and never polished or cherished. Other frequently suggested categories are: an article of clothing, a means of transport, an animal, a food, a plant, a piece of music . . . but there's really no limit. It's a good exercise, but played by yourself it can quickly become rather negative. Much better training is to do it about someone else. A more dangerous version is the Balkan Furniture Game – that's my name for what I first played, one slivovitz-fuelled evening on the banks of the Danube, with a group of writers from across the Balkans. In this version, you pick someone *else* in the group and describe them according to categories everyone else fires at you – until someone guesses who it is. The sooner the better, since that means you're capturing them accurately. It's dangerous, of course, because you're describing someone else who's in the room. You have to do so accurately or no one will guess who it is, but the person being described may not like the images you devise . . . .

A good compromise, if you're working alone, is to pick someone you know and use the Furniture Game to evoke them. If you choose someone close to you – a partner or family member – you can do this on lots of different occasions and your choices will probably differ each time, depending on how you're feeling about them. Precision in similes is always *subjective* precision. It's important to remember this because literary judgement – the author's eye – *is* a matter of personal flair. You aren't a documentary photographer, trying to leave out your own experience and angle on things. On the contrary, you're making the world of your poems come alive through your *own* insights. So the fourth rule of similes is that the more original they are – providing they still *fit* – the more work they will do.

Fifth, though, the simile must be universally available. There's no point in comparing your object to something hardly anybody will be able to get as an *image*. Studding a poem with rare or privileged examples *can* form a valuable part of poetic texture. Geoffrey Hill's poems have suggested the resonance of the archaic, the glamour of the lost, since his early *Mercian Hymns* and *The Songbook of Sebastian Arrurruz*. But such examples are not *images*; they don't do the work of similes. If you tell me 'her eyes were like an agave', I have no idea what you mean. It's a private simile. But if you tell me 'her eyes remind me of the green agave', I begin to get a sense that you are being reminded of something which, presumably, you mean to indicate is *not* here and now. I get the sense of *distance* – and through that of a *rare* green. As for the specifics of its being a Latin American plant – I still won't know that unless I look the word up.

This isn't an argument against bringing rich cultural and geographical experiences into English language poetry. Using objects and vocabulary from the widest range of experiences constantly enriches the language. But that can only happen when those names are used in a public way, not a private one. If this is the first time a word is likely to have been used in an English-language poem then, like a teacher or anyone else who is stretching their listener's vocabulary, you need to give it a little context. It's all right for the reader to look something up, but it's not all right for a poet to mystify deliberately. Using an image because it's there in your experience is part of the healthy synthesis of writing a poem. Trying to find something that will blind your reader with science is symptomatic of some problem in your relationship to that reader – and to poetry, which doesn't talk to itself. The origins of imagery in sympathetic magic show, instead, that the powerful links it makes can be at the centre of human experience.

9 Shape-shifting

I have been many shapes
Before I became Taliesin.

John Fairfax, 'Renewing Riddle'

One of the great pleasures of writing is escape. This is both the most unequivocal of activities – you put whatever it is you have to say *on the record* – and an escape from the fixity of experience. After all, in writing you can make things up.

But much poetry isn't really fiction. Indeed, it's often read as straight autobiography. The Confessional poetry of Robert Lowell, and his pupils Anne Sexton and Sylvia Plath, continues to mark English-language poetry and, especially, expectations of it. The poetry Lowell was writing harnessed the transformative and intensifying power of emotions to bring the world of experience to life. This group of Americans used their emotions as a resource – even, we could say, as an intellectual strategy – to help their poetry resonate. In much the same way, poets from other traditions use the ability of their unconscious to form resonant and dramatic symbols that bring their work alive. The Surrealists, like poets drawing on traditions of hypnosis and shamanism, quite deliberately used their dreaming minds – accessed through dream diaries, 'automatic writing', self-hypnosis or drug and alcohol use – to heighten and strengthen their work. This didn't mean that they were mad and their writing was a pathological symptom. On the contrary, they were *deliberately* exploiting these personal resources.

Of course, it's probably true that poets with pressing personal experience of the power of emotion will be more interested in harnessing it to their work. And maybe writers who dabble in simulating, or stimulating, psychosis are more likely to get stuck with it in some way. As our mothers used to say, if you keep pulling a face, you'll be stuck when the wind changes direction. More than this, though, if distress of some kind – whether it's an exile's longing or a profound mental disorder – is colouring your life, it is likely to be the Big Topic you repeatedly address. Robert Lowell did indeed experience clinical depression. He was repeatedly hospitalized, as was Anne Sexton, who killed herself. As did Sylvia Plath. Lowell, Sexton and Plath all wrote great poetry about the experiences of depression, despair and, especially in Sexton's case, hospitalization. But all three were great poets who *chose* to do so. Another of Lowell's close colleagues, his poetic peer and friend Elizabeth Bishop, also suffered from depression and alcoholism, and experienced suicide at close quarters when her partner killed herself. But Bishop is *not* a Confessional poet. Though she writes about deeply personal themes of memory and experience, her strategy is to harness every faculty that is *not* emotional.

Here, for example, is part of Bishop's poem about existential unsafety, 'In the Waiting Room':

I said to myself: three days
and you'll be seven years old
I was saying it to stop
the sensation of falling off
the round, turning world
into cold, blue-black space.

And here is Anne Sexton, in 'Old':

I'm afraid of needles
I'm tired of rubber sheets and tubes.
I'm tired of faces that I don't know
and now I think that death is starting.

One of the clearest differences between these poems is in their diction. Whereas Bishop's closed-up, perfected prosody makes her sound like an omniscient narrator even as she takes us into the mind of a little girl – and we trust that tone of omniscience – Sexton's *diction*, describing an experience of hospitalization that is in fact terrifyingly adult, could *be* that of a little girl. It is, we might say, deliberately or *faux naïf*. These are technical choices, of register and viewpoint. Two great poets are making artistic *decisions*, not being at the mercy of their pathologies. Poems are literary acts, rather than symptoms; and one of the things that makes them work like this is the stabilizing influence of the implied reader. We'll look at this character in Chapter 16. Meanwhile, it may be worth remembering that a poem, which foregrounds the musical, which is to say oral, elements of language, is *intrinsically* a form of vocal communication. It's their voice in our ear: your voice in their ear.

Poetry is the intimate whisper at the other end of the spectrum from the great public political speech. As we've seen, that doesn't stop it from using rhetoric itself. But it does mean that a poem is a much more flexible, lateral form than political argumentation. The Welsh word for this kind of quality is wonderfully onomatopoeic. *Ystwyth* (pronounced: *ust-whith*) means flexible, winding. As the repeated vowel sounds of *y* and *wy* suggest – getting inside the word and seeming to knead it – it also means malleable. The town of Aberystwyth takes its name from the River Ystwyth, so named because it's a winding lowland river, unusual for that part of the country. The shallow, languid Ystwyth, palpably *making its way* through clay, round lowland grazing, and building up shingle banks – clearly negotiating with its environment, in short – is a model of the flexible and indirect, and of shape-shifting.

Perhaps it's no coincidence that the early poet Taliesin, who according to legend was the son of the shape-shifter Blodeuwedd and himself claims, in an apocryphal but much-loved poem, to be a master of the shape-shift, is said to be buried in Bedd Taliesin, just north of Aberystwyth.

This flexible river, liable to change course from time to time, is a good metaphor for the almost-evasive, yet reactive, character of good poetry: which takes on extra shades of meaning as it needs to, according to the circumstances in which it's read. This flexibility is in fact a sign of *resilience* of meaning. In his *Letters*, Ted Hughes mentions how the alchemists believed that things got most difficult just before a breakthrough. As Paul Simon says, 'The more you near your destination, / The more you go slip-sliding away.' Alchemists pictured these difficulties as a snake. Psycho-analysts talk instead about resistance. They say that the part of the self which doesn't want to relinquish a secret, or a pattern, fights harder as it's cornered. As we've already seen, language becomes less logical and more interrupted by non-semantic elements when people are talking about something that really matters to them.

So a certain snakiness in a poem can be a sign of power, not weakness. This theoretical truth becomes intuitive when we read a teenager's diary, or hear a political slogan. Intuitively we know, however much we respect their sentiments and experience, that these 'full on' texts don't work as poems. They seem untransformed; two-dimensional. And we're right. The snaky, often even sneaky, forces of obliquity and allusion aren't there to add a third dimension of *possibility* to the words.

This doesn't mean we should be writing poems like cross-word puzzles, full of clues and codes. Flexibility within a poem, as both river and snake metaphors suggest, must be living, organic and vital. But it does mean that the true poet can write, as Shakespeare did, wonderfully finished love sonnets in which a 'dark lady' figures: and we don't even know whether it's a man or a woman. Or produce, like Sylvia

Plath, poems that, however much they're scrutinized, don't *explain* her later suicide. Or write pastorals that are really about living in the shadow of approaching death, as Edward Thomas did after he had enlisted.

One of Thomas's poems from that time, 'Lights Out', is both about falling asleep and about dying. It opens:

> I have come to the borders of sleep,
> The unfathomable deep
> Forest where all must lose
> Their way, however straight
> Or winding, soon or late;
> They cannot choose.

This is a poem I've often used in hospice. It can be as much about death as the reader (or, in hospice, the listener) wants it to be. It familiarizes death and makes it something *like* sleep: 'From rest and sleep, which but thy pictures be / Much pleasure, then much more from thee, must flow' as John Donne has it, in Holy Sonnet 10 ('Death be not proud'). Alternatively, it can make sleep wonderfully strange. The dream-border between sleep and death, in imagery drawing on the famous mid-life forest of Dante's journey into the underworld – Thomas was in mid-life when he wrote this – is a 'Wandering Border', as in a poem by the Estonian Jaan Kaplinski. The border, a matter of *naming*, passes over and through the poet.

Working for a long decade in hospitals, hospice, hostels and prisons has shown me how poetry's flexibility makes it an unusually safe form in which to think – and to share that thinking. A poem can be what you want it to be, whether you're a reader or a writer. What's too risky to say directly – in a social situation or even to youself – can be said by a poem that simply doesn't close down on a particular possibility. It can be easier to express vulnerability of all kinds through metaphor, or fiction, than directly. Myth is a great example of this. It's surprising, given the near-universal loss of Classical education in contemporary schools, how many male poets resort to the myth of the hunter Actaeon: who, stumbling on the goddess Artemis naked, shamed her though he didn't mean to. The difficulties of handling male sexuality appropriately – Artemis's revenge is to turn Actaeon into a stag to be torn to pieces by his own hunting dogs – have been explored in recent British poetry by Robin Robertson ('The Death of Actaeon', 'Actaeon: The Early Years'), Neil Rollinson ('Gift'), Ted Hughes ('Actaeon') – and the Welsh woman poet Derryn Rees Jones ('Quiver'). These poems open up a space in which to think as much about contemporary actions as about Greek myth. Find them and read them. You'll notice how engaging their arguments become when fleshed out in characterization.

In the poem attributed to Taliesin, it's not only the poem but the poet himself who can shape-shift. The use of poetry in times of stress has become fashionable in the UK. It takes the form of everything from themed anthologies to arts-funded hospital writing workshops. There are books on therapeutic journal writing, holistic writing courses, and many occupational therapists and psychotherapists use writing activities, including poetry, in their work. Of course, writing poetry isn't automatically therapeutic. Too many great, productive poets, from Chatterton to John Berryman, have killed themselves for this to be the case. Poets aren't, as a group, conspicuously high-functioning members of society. Many people who are very disturbed write almost obsessively. Their poems can take on talismanic properties, and get carried around in handbag or jacket pocket. And yet poetry, like all writing, *does* allow us to imagine another reality. In this way it allows us to reinvent ourselves. When nothing else can be controlled, what's on the page *can* be: providing we have enough technique, time and attention to give it.

Talent matters, too. But the great thing about writing is that talent and seeing what's required are the same thing. The mediocre run-of-the-mill poet stops because he simply doesn't notice that his poem is banal, and needs either more electric language or more hard-won insight. The poet who realizes that her poem's flabby or dull has the insight – the *ability* – to make it something more exciting.

Writing a poem, then, can be a species of self-invention. It can also be a kind of self-discovery. Like everything else to do with poetry, that discovery may lead to something which is under-defined rather than schematic. After all, if you can fully itemize what a fascinating person you are in a poem, you probably already had this in mind before you decided to write. That's obviously not the same as exploring what you don't yet know. The American poet Adrienne Rich, in her sequence about poem-making, calls this self-exploration 'Diving into the Wreck'. However, the *dive,* into whatever the poem turns out to be, takes place in every piece of writing you do; and it has nothing to do with autobiography. In fact, that genre is less likely to lead to self-exploration because it approaches its questions directly, by way of narrative facts: the level at which you already know about yourself.

Indirectness – Emily Dickinson's 'tell the whole truth but tell it slant' – is no literary secret. William Empson's *Seven Types of Ambiguity* identified forms of flexibility that brought literary writing to life. Another highly influential critical book, M.H. Abrams's *The Mirror and the Lamp* (1953), points out that while writing may simply reflect a picture of the world, at its best it will illuminate that whole world with a particular *understanding*. Illumination, and its softening shadows, is an image of *flexible clarity*. Indeed, metaphors in general – with their space for unpacking and interpretation and yet their internal consistency – are models of how flexible clarity can be achieved. This chapter, for example, has relied on them precisely because it's looking at something that is hard to *explain*.

How, apart from reading for examples, do we find the flexibility and shape-shifting potential in our own writing? There are a number of ways. Each, suitably enough, is rather indirect. The first is to practise *writing without explanation*. Haiku are, at their best, juxtapositions of image 'facts' that work by *staging* their logic. The Classical haiku has three lines with a fixed number of syllables: 5–7–5. It also contains an image from the season it is written in, an image from the natural world, *and* an image of mutability. The three-line haiku stages an arrival at the necessity of occurrence, a 'turn'. It shows what is happening. Probably Basho's most famous haiku, translated by Robert Hass (without syllable count: this is a translation, after all), is:

The old pond –
a frog jumps in,
sound of water.

One single image may perform all three roles: the frog is seasonal, natural *and* changing. But seasonal images don't have to be from the natural world (they do have to be *images*, though: frozen pipes, unlike icicles hanging by the wall, are a fact you tell us about, not something we can be shown). What is essential to the haiku is the apparently affectless impingement of its elements on each other. They aren't joined with explanatory conjunctions: *so, but, later.* The haiku works all as one piece.

As well as writing without explanation, *writing without naming* – in a riddle, for example – is good practice for developing flexible clarity. Practise characterizing places and people with sets of qualities from all five senses. The River Ystwyth is the smell of damp pines, the sound of a raven quacking overhead, and so on. Or use the Furniture Game: 'If I were a river I'd be the Ystwyth, perfectly transparent and yet always getting away from you', etc. It's easy to turn this material into a riddle using the 'I am' formula: 'I am the underground smell of pine, / The raven quacking above your head'. To go further with this, you could return to the exercises in Chapter 3 in order to experiment with writing in different personae.

Flexibility is close to subtlety. In good writing, which pays attention to flexibility of meaning and diction, poetic ambiguity is carefully and delicately constructed. It's one of the things that most clearly marks poetry's difference from prose. In the next chapter, we look more closely at the other side of this aspect of poetics: the clarity that goes alongside flexibility.

10 Clarity

Pearl, pleasant to prince's pay
To cleanly close in gold so clear

Pearl (trans. Victor Watts)

Perhaps the most unexpected thing a poem needs is clarity. Because it's made of language, poetry is at heart grammatical, logical and self-explanatory. The popular idea that it should be 'difficult', a by-product of a high level of education, or mysterious, is a misconception. It's true that poetry is exceptional. Its language already works exceptionally hard in order to do several things at once: these include patterning, beautifying, and exploring complex topics in greater depth than most prose. In fact, it has to be extra clear because of all this. To imagine that words and phrases should make *less* sense when they're used in a poem is a bit like believing that the lyrics of a song can be less clear than unaccompanied text. On the contrary, they need to be clearer to communicate *through* the music.

Clarity is most easily learnt by example, and it's hard to study without taking your own poems *as* that example. So in this chapter you'll work on your poetry as if you were an editor. You'll be looking at the four areas where muddle can occur: *grammar*, *diction*, *image* and *argument*.

The idea of clarity isn't to produce poems that are flatly explanatory, but to allow them to ring 'clear as a bell'. A cracked bell, sounding more than one note at a time, *smudges* itself, whereas a poem's multiplicity of ideas and meanings works because of the way it has been *brought together* and *aligned* so that everything resonates together. For example, in 'The Voice', an apparently simple poem by Thomas Hardy, several layers of meaning and music are going on at once, but they are in tune with one another. 'Woman much missed, how you call to me, call to me', this poem addresses the poet's late wife, ending, 'Wind oozing thin through the thorn from norward, / And the woman calling.' The poem's shift from second to third person, as if to suggest the ghost receding, is echoed by the shift from a rather energetic dactylic line to end on the darker trochaic metre, with its dragged foot. In addition, that *oo / or / all* assonance draws the sound of wind- and ghost-call through the ending.

Elsewhere, Don Paterson's version of one of Rainer Maria Rilke's *Sonnets to Orpheus* seems simple because of its clarity of diction: 'From star to star – such distances: and yet / those we encounter here are harder reckoned' ('Distance'). But these ideas are complex, and without the accompanying clarity they could become off-putting. We'll look at translation and what it teaches *every* poet, including the non-linguist, in Chapter 15. Meanwhile, however, the question is how to achieve clarity in your own work. The answer is that you need to test out your poems in a number of ways.

I Grammar

The first and most fundamental test has to do with *grammatical construction*. Read through your most complex poems to date and ask yourself whether every sentence is a full grammatical entity. Is there a subject, an active verb and – generally speaking – an object? A typical poetic tic is the sentence with no active verb: 'The weather in the streets.' 'The way I long for you.' Also typical is the sentence as a gathering of clauses to no explicitly related end. Thus: 'It was after the longing, the gathering, the picking of apples'. *That – what?* one wants to ask. Typical too is opening a paired or balancing statement – 'She was both the one person he wanted to see more than anyone in the world, and he wanted to see her soon' – without closing or balancing it.

All three of these classic grammatical smudges seem to have arisen when the writer lost her way in a thought. The more expansive your sub-clauses, the easier this is to do. Long, compendious sentences that evoke feeling-the-way, or a richness of scene, are particularly risky; and yet can be the most successful when they're reined-in by accurate grammar. However, sometimes the way gets lost not just in *the middle* of the sentence but because we smudge the grammatical construction from the outset. In my third example, 'She was both the one person he wanted to see more than anyone in the world, and he wanted to see her soon', it may not be that the writer has left off the balancing statement – 'And at the same time the source of more exasperation than he had ever thought possible'. It may be, rather, that the 'both' isn't a pivot between two contrasted statements but an intensifier that wants to apply itself to the subsidiary clause, 'and he wanted to see her soon'. (It's just the wrong term, in other words.) Maybe this student of the human heart meant something like, 'She was the one person he wanted to see more than anyone in the world, and *moreover* he wanted to see her soon.'

One of the reasons that translation is such a good discipline is that it demands that we at least *know what the poem means* grammatically. The old belief that, in poetry, word order *should* be disrupted is clumsy. Though only a tyro would be happy with the pseudo-archaic 'To Worthing I must go' rather than 'I must go to Worthing', poetic word order does get jumbled up more than seems quite fair. It was alright for Wordsworth to write 'We walk'd along, while bright and red / Uprose the morning sun', in 'Two April Mornings': it wouldn't sound so good in a new poem. One of the best defences against this is simply to train the ear to hear this sort of thing as positively ugly, rather than vaguely attractive. The aesthetic conscience is the best ally of the grammatical ear.

Look out greetings card verse, songs and poems from minor nineteenth-century anthologies, for examples of what I call *kitsch grammar*. After spending a while with this stuff, you realize it's alright to laugh and, using that laughter as a cue, to resist it. After all, a contemporary marketeer charged with promoting slow food and organic produce would cringe at the fake beams and mass-produced chintz of the 1970s version of *Ye Olde Englande*.

As Lynne Truss has demonstrated, hunting out punctuation *faux pas* is fun too. The most common lacuna is simply not closing parenthetical commas. We tend to use the comma as a speech-mark, indicating a pause or a phrase. But this is often lazy. Too many commas spoil the broth. The hard-working comma is never merely ornamental it is but structural. In an over-comma'd text whatever work commas *do* achieve is often lost, because it's impossible for the reader to know which pairs off with which. This mark either separates elements in a list, even a discursive and expansive one, or brackets off a phrase. It can also separate a balanced pair of statements. Sometimes that's hard to see, as when a phrase is also part-bracketed by the start or end of a sentence. Often, too, there's more than one dependent clause – a phrase that *needs* bracketing – in a sentence. If you use commas for each, you muddle them with each other. It's possible to use dashes around one such clause instead. Similarly, when a sentence needs both large and small divisions, semi-colons provide a greater degree of separation. One rule of thumb is that, where a sentence could grammatically – if not semantically or aesthetically – be divided into shorter sentences, a semi-colon might do the job instead.

What has this to do with poetry? Everything. A poem is *harder* to read than prose. The eye may *eventually* be helped by line-breaks, but at first reading they are simply additional information to be processed. Poetry is a language of compression, yet many fine poems use very long sentences – some are even comprised entirely of a single sentence. While lineation can become a form of extra punctuation, allowing the poet to keep a flexible sentence aloft, the pressures such poems impose on punctuation are considerable. An over-punctuated poem looks fussy and rebarbative. W.S. Merwin says that a full-stop 'staples' a poem to the page. Yet an under-punctuated poem can easily be unclear, because the temptation is to use *the ear* – the *music* of lineation – to inflect the sentence and give it sense. But the reader won't have the author on hand to read them the poem. They need to be able to work out both sense and rhythm from *what's on the page*.

Here are some punctuation pointers I use as a checklist, especially when working with the kind of long, complex material that easily gets out of hand:

1 Be consistent. Don't use commas for part of a list, or to open a parenthesis, and a line-break to continue that list or close the parenthesis.

2 No more than one colon per sentence. A colon is the sentence 'opening its hands' in *a showing gesture*. Either it shows a balancing statement, or it introduces a subsidiary structure, such as a list. We can't 'open' such subsidiary statements *back* to general sentence level.

3 Avoid the Oxford comma (the one before the *and* at the end of a list) except in emergencies.

4 Aim to let the musculature of the poem, which is to say its *poetic* structures, do the work for you. For example, if you have a set of alternating clauses, are you sure you want to syncopate them *across* the line-breaks in a series of enjambments? Is that part of their internal logic – a kind of push-me-pull-you, for example – or just fashion? Could you use the line-breaks instead?

5 If you decide to be radical with punctuation, for example by not using full stops but only capital letters (or vice versa), are you sure your poem not only justifies but *entails* this radical language act? There's a recent fashion for omitting the final full stop from British poems. Especially in the case of sonnets, which build towards the *closure* of their final couplet, this omission generates a radical sense of open-endedness. But is

your poem truly open-ended? Or do you just think it looks cool to under-punctuate? Elsewhere, writing that models itself on Beat poetry often omits capital letters. This can work well with stream-of-consciousness, and in fleeting, demotic verse. It doesn't work nearly so well with abstraction, or poems distorted by lots of proper names.

6   *Stop, look, listen*: is that comma really necessary?

II Diction

Diction is, at least in part, a surprising corollary of grammatical clarity. The poetic ideal isn't a grey drizzle of words but lucidity, a bright day. This is true whether the poem is a profoundly layered and culturally resonant work from someone like Peter Porter or Amy Clampitt, a strongly coloured confessional by a new young poet, or comes from the heart of the lyric tradition. The equivalents in diction of the overused comma are: the repetitive article (the, a), unnecessary conjunctions (so, because, therefore), and excessive resort to the various simile constructions (like, as if, it seemed, the way that). Each has its roots, paradoxically, in the desire to clarify. But such an explanatory urge is very different from simply inserting necessary punctuation. Properly punctuated, the words you've chosen for a poem can do the work they need to. Explanations, on the other hand, stop them from working because, by showing that even the poet doesn't trust what's written to stand up by itself, they undermine it. Besides, words like 'the' and 'because' are dulled by use. They're a kind of packaging, which gets in the way as much as it protects.

III Image

We drag in explanation in order to bolster up an image that we're not sure works. *Because* and *as if* are like builders' scaffolding retroactively underpinning a house: for example, when a metaphor needs to be *extended*. In fact, the sustained, stretched-out metaphor isn't, as its name suggests, somehow *going beyond* its natural span. It's simply avoiding both making a too-quick appearance and subsiding into the contradiction of mixed metaphor. Consider the virtuoso extended metaphor of Robert Frost's 'The Road Not Taken', where that road is both concrete and existential:

> Two roads diverged in a yellow wood,
> And sorry I could not travel both
> And be one traveller, long I stood
> And looked down one as far as I could
> To where it bent in the undergrowth;

Another extended metaphor – one which, far from being allowed to contradict itself or trail away within the poem, explores every aspect, bringing it more and more to life – occurs in Shakespeare's 'Sonnet 29':

> When, in disgrace with Fortune and men's eyes,
> I all alone beweep my outcast state,
> And trouble deaf heaven with my bootless cries,
> And look upon myself and curse my fate,
> Wishing me like to one more rich in hope,
> Featured like him, like him with friends possessed,
> Desiring this man's art, and that man's scope,
> With what I most enjoy contented least,
> Yet in these thoughts myself almost despising,
> Haply I think on thee, and then my state,
> Like to the lark at break of day arising
> From sullen earth, sings hymns at heaven's gate
>
> For thy sweet love remembered such wealth brings,
> That then I scorn to change my state with kings.

The idea of listening or hearing is so wittily explored in the poem that this metaphor is less an image than a *conceit*. In other words, it's not so much a *representation* of something concrete, as one *idea* applied to another. This is metaphor as parable: telling a story about how something that can't be directly perceived by the senses would work if it were put in place of the original object of poetic scrutiny. A recent poet who takes such a conceit and works it out to the nth degree – often to the point of absurdity – is Wislawa Szymborska. Her poems tend to inhabit a metaphor and then – in her own version of 'the turn' – take off with it into that metaphor's own logic. Szymborska, previously published by the tiny independent Forest Books, became widely available in the UK once she won the Nobel Prize for Literature.

Clarity doesn't necessarily require images or metaphors to be extended, but it does need them to stand up to the same level of testing-to-destruction that Szymborska deploys. Are they consistent? Believable? Just as the proof of true characterization in fiction is that the reader is able to imagine the character in *more* situations than those actually given, so in poetry image, metaphor, even turn of phrase, must not contradict themselves or each other, but remain believable in some way up to and beyond the end of the poem. Generally speaking, that simply requires attention to continuity. This is particularly true of times of day and other geophysical details, such as the weather. Attention to pronouns is important, too. If there's an omniscient narrator, who would 'we' be? If 'you' is used to mean 'one', it can't *also address* an individual.

Another important failure of continuity occurs when a symbolic value changes from positive to negative (or vice versa) within a poem. Poems can accommodate these kinds of shift as narrative development, but they must *be* shifts, not slippage. Unless there's a great deal of circumstantial, or supporting, evidence in the poem, the writer often needs to *insert* explicit structures around them. This explicitness may take the form of temporal or spatial conjunctions: 'later', 'behind it'; or conceptual conjunctions, such as 'on the other hand' or 'nevertheless'. Shifts can also be enabled by the insertion of *narrative explanation* – in effect a *because*, making explicit the two points between which movement happens: for example, 'since you've gone' and 'because the weather turned'.

IV Argument

Of these potential losses of clarity, the most problematic are those where a symbolic value shifts too radically. Such shifts can relate to a slippage in mood or atmosphere – in the emotional message, or argument, of the poem. Though a poem can express more than one thing, it needs to express each clearly: alongside (or before or after) every other. An elegy can show *both* the hurt *and* the anger that are part of loss. The former American poet laureate Donald Hall's wonderful books written after the death of his wife, such as *The Painted Bed*, do so across whole sequences. However, the compass of such writing must be set with precision in order not to confuse, for example, anger at the cause of death with anger at the person who has disappeared. Within the poem, a persona – even a narrator – may well confuse these two: the poet must not. A similar risk of smudge might be run by a poem about an ex-lover. It's an accomplished poet who can move between longing, tenderness and sarcasm, without conflating them.

In short, *ambivalence* – a quality of poetic narrative – is not the same as *ambiguity*. Just as a poem must 'earn' its emotion by showing, not telling, as the useful cliché goes, so any shift or unevenness in tone must 'earn its keep' through a corresponding development or shift in what the poem says. I may be ambivalent about the religion I was brought up in – I may even write a poem which explores the mixture of compassion and stringency that I believe characterized it, leaving room for a reader to draw their own conclusions about this paradox – but I would have failed if my poem portrayed compassion and stringency as undifferentiated from each other; or if the reader didn't know what I was comparing. If my poem is ambiguous, it creates no space *for* ambivalence, or any other poetic experience.

So how do we separate and protect the elements in a poem? It comes down to *fulfilling intention*. But this isn't the same as writing a poem as if by recipe: knowing beforehand what all the ingredients will be, the order they'll be used in, and the likely result. It's the poem's *own* intention that must be fulfilled. The draft poem is a sequence of thoughts proceeding, according to their own logic, to some conclusion. Some of this logic will be dictated by grammar, some by diction or register – an understated poem has a particular relationship to emotional drama, for example – and some will result from image-logic. Once you've introduced the image of an umbrella, say, certain metaphorical steps (having to do with weather) become more likely than others (such as moving on to soft furnishings). However, the poem's musculature, the way it proceeds, is achieved primarily through thoughts reacting to one another.

Thought that's strong enough to connect two insights will tug on and may distort them. An under-developed thought is a passenger, and often a smudge, on those surrounding it. The *argument* is the order of thought in a poem, and it must be *both* internally logical and worth making. If it is, then image, diction and grammar should only ever need superficial adjustment, since they can rely on the *order* of thought to find their way back to where they were trying to go.

It's surprising how often emerging poets fail to examine their poems for logic. Yet this necessary step is easy to do. Take a recent poem – but not one you've been working on so recently that you know the words off by heart – and ask yourself, at the end of each phrase or line: 'What does this mean? What did I *want* it to mean? Does it relate to what comes before and after?' If each phrase survives this inquisition, and if they add up to something whose *argument* you could paraphrase, then you have a well-made poem.

If not: be ruthless. However much you love a line, if it's doing no work in *this* poem – or is working in the wrong direction – take it out. It may be a fine phrase – but it's not *right*, here. Paste it in a notebook. I keep a 'drafts' document open on the computer all the time I'm revising. This way, you don't feel you've lost what you put aside, and you will be more radical with your cuts. Even a phrase that is wonderfully to the point may not fit where you've placed it. It might really be the poem's starting point or conclusion, or the start of a whole other poem. To test out your nose for this, take two or three of your favourite lines from poets you admire, and slot them into your poem. Now you should be able to see that they can be both marvellous, and absolutely wrong for your poem, at the same time. This is particularly likely to be true of any of your *own* phrases you're particularly pleased with. Those are probably the very ones that have least to do with their neighbours, and that you test least rigorously. Suspect yourself!

Despite all the make-up in the world, what matters most is good bone structure. Your poems will emerge from this testing process both clearer – *and* more beautiful.

11 To rhyme or not to rhyme?

The word bites like a fish.

Stephen Spender, 'Word'

It's the most frequent objection to contemporary poetry. It's made headlines so many times it's not even newsworthy. And still it comes, over and over: *poetry doesn't rhyme any more.* Close behind marches the corollary: *and if it doesn't rhyme, how do you know it's poetry?*

Perhaps this is the fault of once-upon-a-time classrooms. Until the 1960s, at least, pupils had to memorize long passages of poetry; it's not surprising, then, that teachers picked rhyming verse, with its built-in cues for memory. Besides, narrative verse, often thought to be the place children should start, tends to rhyme. From ballads to Longfellow's *Hiawatha* to Vikram Seth's verse-novel in sonnets, *Golden Gate*, strict form is often part of what unifies a longer, story-telling poem. Strict metre, the foundation on which strict rhyme is built, keeps a longer piece moving – just as march time or a dance beat are designed to keep things moving along.

Traditional full rhyme is also thought to appeal directly to children, because it makes the poem 'portable'. It seems to 'contain' the verse, giving it ready-made boundaries and an identity. And, of course, even today a good teacher hopes his or her pupils will 'catch on to' classroom poems, remember them, and start quoting them at home or in the playground. Underlying this is the sensible perception that most of us, as children, loved *playing with sound*. Our language-alert ears found rhyme so easy it was almost hard to resist. Think of the nonsense rhymes you inherited or made up in the schoolyard. Everything from parody to name-calling was easy because you simply stepped sideways through rhyme. In fact, children are so addicted to rhyming that, in schools' workshops, it can be hard to *stop* them using it. Teenagers move naturally into rap and performance poetry because that musical, aural sense of the possibilities of rhyme is still with them.

'Besides,' the child's-eye view goes, 'Who can tell whether something's *poetic* enough? But you know you've done something specific when you rhyme.' It's easy to remember back to your own classroom encounters with poems – the ones that were supposed to make you laugh, or those that were *about describing* – and how off-putting they were. But everyone gets nostalgic for the familiar as they get older. That's why so many people who don't usually have anything to do with poetry resort, when they do think about it, to the comfortably predictable, *rhyming* poems of their youth.

And rhyme *is* a handrail through the complexities and emotions with which poetry often deals. It can also be an addiction, a complex challenge that has become an end in itself. At best, it's a kind of virtuosity. At worst, it's an escape from real poem-making into an easy jingle of words that pretty much generate themselves. I often suspect it's the anxiously-achieving child, the one who rhymed in order to 'make sure they were doing it right', speaking when adults maintain contemporary poetry is nothing because it doesn't rhyme. 'How do you know it's a poem if it doesn't rhyme?' is in fact the same question as, 'How do you know it's a poem?' The answers to both have to do with the action of poetry upon the reader. You know it's a poem because it offers you what you come to poetry for: certainty or mystery, comfort or enchantment, beauty or challenge. Poetry is part of the culture of every time and place. In many of those places and times it hasn't rhymed, certainly not with regular full rhyme at the end of every line, however replete it may have been with other structures, from the assonance of Welsh *cynghanedd* (more on this later) to the fixed metre of dub.

So I suggest we turn this prejudice inside out. Rhyme is a *manifestation* of poetic qualities, such as order, form and beauty, rather than being such a quality *itself*. It may manifest beautifully sometimes, but at others as unpleasant mindlessness. And here's another way to be sure that the complainers are wrong: a great deal of contemporary British poetry *does* rhyme. Most of our important and influential poets, from Don Paterson to Alan Jenkins, move in and out of rhyme. The mainstream is *not* turning away from it: in fact, if anything there's more rhyme there than in the poetic margins, which sometimes linger in a 1970s free verse sensibility, or with post-modern and language poetry. I remember, when I'd been editing *Poetry Review* for about a year, getting a letter of complaint from a member of the Poetry Society. The *Review*, he complained, was publishing nothing that rhymed. It so happened that the issue he was complaining about included twelve sonnets, a villanelle, a ballad and one other rhyming poem, all fifteen of them in strict rhyme, out of a little under forty poems. In short, this correspondent (who turned out not to be unusual) could not or would not *read* the actual poetry he was complaining about.

I think this has to do with fear. If you don't have the handrail of strict form as a guide, you have to be open to a poem and see what experience it gives you: what it *does* to you. That requires courage, for poetry *can* stray into difficult metaphysical or emotional territory. Indeed, at its best, it conducts one of T.S. Eliot's 'raids on the inarticulate', bringing back something we've never before been able to put into words: even if only about the character of a red wheelbarrow (as in the William Carlos Williams poem).

So rhyme can be a sign of poetic conservatism, but it can

also be the opposite: the safety-rail that allows the poem to take real risks. Rilke's *Sonnets to Orpheus*, and the English Metaphysical poets including Thomas Traherne and Henry Vaughan, provide examples of poetry that can go as far as it does conceptually *because* it is held together by the formal language of rhyme. Rhyme can also work, at its best, as a generator of new, exciting choices one would never have made without its particular pressures, and which open up whole new areas of meaning and imagination in a subject.

Like any other technique, though, rhyme needs us to display fluency before it will do this for us. Rhyme is a muscle that needs to be developed. It's at its most obvious in maximum volume *full rhyme* at the ends of lines (*end-rhyme*); it structures a poem by working through the reader's ear at both a conscious and an unconscious level when it's embedded within the lines – *internal rhyme*; and it is at its most sophisticated in *half-rhyme*, the kind that seems like an echo or a failure, compromised or subtle, and which is often no more than assonance.

I Full rhyme

Let's start with full rhyme. Just because it *is* full – two lines, whether or not they're consecutive, rhyme without any complexity inflecting that rhyme – doesn't mean it has to be slavish or dull. Elizabeth Bishop was the mistress of the cheeky rhyme. 'One Art' has:

> I lost my mother's watch. And look! <u>my last, or</u>
> next-to-last, of three loved houses went.
> The art of losing isn't hard to <u>master</u>

And here two more examples of rhymes that seem as if they ought not to work – which are ill-matched to the eye – from Alan Jenkins:

With darkness by six <u>there comes</u>
Not the odour of sunless chrysan<u>themums</u>

('Talking to the Undertaker')

. . . we were in love, *au bord de la mer* . . .
But the leaves whispered, 'Are you still that <u>suburban</u>
Boy who dreamed of taking opium with Baudelaire
Or wine with Byron, of setting sail from Greenwich to <u>Durban</u>

('Salt')

These 'category-error' rhymes add spice because their *unexpectedness* doubles the aural pleasure. It's enjoyable to rehearse the chiming rhymes of 'there comes' and 'chrysan-themums', or *'au bord de l[a m]er'* and 'Baudelaire': but even more enjoyable to have them leap out of their textual disguise. What makes them work is precisely that, however they *look*, they *sound* full rhyme. In fact, the disjunction between eye and ear makes them sound even more clearly. On the other hand, a technical smudge – for example rhyming 'comes' with 'pines', even though this would make the eye happier – would make the sound less clear. It would demand the reader's energy rather than *supplying* energy to the poem.

Interestingly, once you have the sounds of the syllables straight, it's *metre* that makes full rhyme chime. In Chapter 4 we looked at the difference between a *masculine* and a *feminine* ending. The masculine ends with a stress; the feminine is unstressed. This is why *unkind* rhymes with *the blinds*, but *happy* (feminine) doesn't rhyme with *a pea* (masculine). Rhyme cannot interrupt metre, which will trample over and distort any word that disrupts its own pattern. Try saying this unpo-etic couplet aloud:

Little Tom was none too happy –
Fish and chips but not one green pea.

Quite apart from its stink of Patronizing Rhymes for Kids, the reversal from trochee to iamb for the last foot of the second line simply doesn't get a look in. Instead, we distort 'green pea', making it sound like 'Greenpeace'. Although, as we've already seen, metre can be refreshed by the alexandrine project – the dot-and-carry-one of an additional foot to break up its regularity – the place for this extra foot, or indeed the extra syllable that often signifies a metrical deviation (for example to make diction more speech-like), *isn't within the rhyme cluster*. Using the same words to do both rhyme and rhythmic disruption would be like using the tent-pole as a spare tent-peg. Using *anything else* will make the structure stronger, but *this* weakens it. If we go back to the Jenkins examples, we can see this metrical regularity in action. In fact, we see it's the metre that *delivers* the rhyme. One of the best ways to practise this is simply to get into the habit of thinking up rhyming pairs of words while you're doing the washing up/in a traffic jam/at the Post Office. Try, in particular, to think up rhymes for words of more than one syllable, paying attention to where the stresses fall as you do so.

One genre that absolutely exploits the resources of full rhyme is the limerick. Going round the room or pub table or car making up instant limericks on a line-a-turn-basis is also great practice, in the right company. Limericks work best when they transgress. Kids love limericks, because their frequent referral to bodily functions is rendered explosive by a rhyme that seems equally transgressive since it's usually so unexpected. They're a great example of how 'category-error' rhyme leaps the psychic tracks. The famous formality of the first line – 'There was a young lady of . . .' – is subverted by its own predication of the wicked rhymes that follow. 'Adult' limericks – the smutty ones (you read it here first) beloved of British male poets, combining technical finesse with other of their preoccupations – work in just the same way. One of the pleasures of making them up is the sense of possibility in the most mundane of place-names. There's a story about the mathematical genius on his death-bed still fascinated by the number of the cab in which his friend arrived to visit him, and able to find all sorts of mathematical patterns and beauty within it. Place-names could be the poet's equivalent. It's good practice to test out even apparently banal parts of language for hidden poetic capacity, and limericks force you to do so because their form is so uncompromising. Here is a kids' classic in place of anything more risqué:

> There was a young lady of Ryde
> Who ate too many apples and died.
> The apples fermented
> Inside the lamented
> And made cider inside her inside.

Limericks are an intrinsically oral form, and so they exploit aurality: I've found that punning last line deeply satisfying ever since I was about seven.

II Internal rhyme

This also brings us nicely on to internal rhyme, where full rhyme happens away from the ends of lines. It may work *with* those line-ends, as in the famous line from Coleridge's 'Rime of the Ancient Mariner' – 'Instead of a cross, the Albatross' – or with other internal rhymes. This is what the ghazal does, as we'll see in Chapter 13.

In other words, it observes the codes of metre in just the same way as an end rhyme does. If anything, it lets the ear subvert the eye even more successfully.

III Half-rhyme

But internal rhyme isn't always full. Here's an example of half-rhyme in the middle of a line:

> The shrill, demented choirs of wailing shells;
> And bugles calling / for them from sad shires.

Significantly, this is from the Welsh poet Wilfred Owen's 'Anthem for Doomed Youth'. Here is the contemporary Welsh poet Gwyneth Lewis's version of the same technique – ' 'Dy benelin yw *elbow*, dy wallt di yw *hair*, // *Chin* yw di ên di, *head* yw dy ben' (italics are in the original). Her internal rhymes occur in the lines that actually quote Welsh, in this (English-language) poem about language-learning: as if the Welsh language brings with it its own poetics. For many such internal half-rhymes are the legacy of the assonantal forms that structured early poetry in the indigenous languages of the British Isles, including Anglo-Saxon and Welsh. Their influence can be traced in the work of, for example, Gerard Manley Hopkins.

Hopkins studied in a seminary in North Wales and became interested in the systematic Welsh patterns of assonance known as *cynghanedd* or *sounding together*. He is famous for his close attention to the work of vowel sounds. He was particularly interested in ordering them not by assonance, however, but by pitch – he called this 'vowelling on' and 'vowelling off' – as here, where 'The Windhover' ascends by 'vowelling off'. You need to read this aloud to get the sense of how the vowels sound in sequence: o – e – a – i and, again, u – o – e – a – i:

> ... in his riding
> Of the <u>rolling level underneath him steady air, and striding</u>
> High there, how he <u>rung upon the rein of a wimpling wing</u>
> In his ecstasy!

'Vowelling on', of course, descends through corresponding vowel pitches in the opposite order (e – a – o – u):

> But we dream we are rooted in earth – *Dust!*
> ('Wreck of the Deutschland')

Hopkins's poetry uses assonance in a very different way from that of traditional forms. It aligns these sounds with the sense of the poem, so that the vowels seem to travel in the same direction as the verse. On the other hand, *cynghanedd*, like other residually oral forms that could be sung or chanted, is a somewhat static music, an embroidery that reifies the couplet rather than moving the poem on. *Cynghanedd* matches the stressed and unstressed syllables in paired half-lines in a series of cross-patterns, which draw the ear and meaning over the half-line break but not necessarily beyond that. These traditional forms employ set named patterns. A couplet keeps to one such pattern. Here's an example of *Cyghanedd Groes* (cross *cynghanedd*), which repeats the consonants in order in each half-line (*w* and *y* are vowels in Welsh) from the medieval poet Dafydd ap Gwilym:

Deg lwyswawd, o'i dy glaswydr

('The Mistle Thrush')

And here's *Cynghanedd Lusg* (dragged *cynghanedd*, in which the penultimate syllable – this example isn't exact! – rhymes with another from earlier in the line):

Clais mawr uwch *garth, tarth* y tir

('The Mist')

This has much in common with the form he used most often, *Cynghanedd Sain*, sound *cynghanedd*, in which the first two parts of a three-part line rhyme and the third alliterates with a word in the second part of the line:

Dros fyn*ydd*, gwyr crefydd Cred

('Girls of Llanbadarn')

As a result of their uses of assonance, Hopkins and ap Gwilym share a richness of texture. What seems breathless and liturgical in Hopkins produces the kind of density that suggests poetic necessity in ap Gwilym. Writing surprisingly secular verse, he was also pushing the limits of Welsh language itself, just as his slightly younger contemporary

Geoffrey Chaucer pushed Middle English to do more than had previously seemed possible.

Assonance gives a sense of internal logic to a line. The more formal the rules it follows, the tighter that logic will bind the verse. Strict rules may seem hard to follow, but once they're mastered, they can produce a poem that truly has the courage of its convictions. Rhyme is a particularly good antidote to too much free-verse. It acts as a check and balance. Is your free-verse really generating its own form? Or is it getting loose and slick? *Cynghanedd* not only demands great linguistic ingenuity: it also requires both poet and reader to *spend longer with* each half-line.

Of course, not all half-rhyme is assonantal. As its name suggests, *slant rhyme* comes in at an aural tangent:

> Jock, away and tell it to the <u>bees</u>:
> they're closing down the facto<u>ry</u>.
> The Post Office women s<u>ay</u>:
> is that old Jock? we thocht he was d<u>ei</u>d!
> > (Kathleen Jamie, 'Jocky in the Wilderness')

This is probably my own favourite form of rhyme: because it is so playful; because it can be used to vary a sequence of full rhyme; and because it introduces a kind of plangency into the language of the poem. Like a chromatic note, or the quartertone pitches of traditional music, it is unsettling and challenging, but never sloppy. I often find myself deliberately replacing the chimingly obvious, 'loud' full rhyme, which a line seems to demand, with a slant rhyme which seems more subtle *both* musically and in meaning. In other words, slant rhymes are often *more* carefully sought after than full rhymes.

The best practice for rhyming is to take an end-rhymed poem you don't know well (but use a contemporary one, so you're not tempted into archaism or inversion). Blank out the line-ends (just use a piece of paper – it's in your own interest not to cheat, after all) and replace them. Do this first of all with full rhyme. How closely do your choices correspond to the

119

original? Are they ever better? Now introduce some half-rhyme. Finally, change some of the end-rhymes to slant rhyme. As you do this with two or three poems, you'll find you begin to get a sense of where half-rhyme can be 'carried', and where slant rhyme underlines the poem's sense. Half-rhyme works well in the middle of a stanza, or sentence, to draw things together. Slant rhyme can introduce the 'turn' in a poem's meaning, or an unexpected concept: or it can throw the reader off the scent at the start of a poem.

There are a couple of rules to make for yourself. Never finish a poem that is otherwise all full rhyme with a half-rhyme or slant rhyme – unless the whole point of the last line is a souring of everything that went before. Generally, the way to demonstrate how in charge of your material you are is to be at your *highest* technical pitch at the poem's summation. Nor should you start a poem with full technical control and then let it go. Unless you're introducing the idea of loss (or gain) of control in what the poem *says*, it's also not a good idea to have all the full rhyme at one end or the other. It's likely to read like the kind of poem written by children and beginners, in which a spontaneous full rhyme suddenly gives up – or gets going – halfway through. Poetry is voluntary human creation, not spontaneous generation, and readers get genuine pleasure from evidence of technique. However, rules aside, the principles for using rhyme are really just the same as those for writing any verse. It's important to have fun and to let your imagination and intellect have full rein – to be as original and creative as possible. Rhyming *is* fun and – rather like other human pleasures – providing it doesn't become an addiction it is life- and poetry-enhancing.

12 High and low: register

O ye'll tak' the high road, and I'll tak' the low road
And I'll be in Scotland afore ye.

Anon, 'The Bonnie Banks of Loch Lomon'

One of the ways we convey most clearly what we mean is through register. It's the linguistic equivalent of body language; the mood-music with which we say what we do. Spoken language has two kinds of register: the literally musical register of pitch, and the semantic register of vocabulary. Poetry can't rely on the pitch of a speaking voice, because even oral traditions have many different speakers. It has to achieve register entirely through its choice of words.

Some people have high, some low, voices. In general, low (masculine) voices are heard as more authoritative than higher ones. A low voice is sexy and worldly; a high voice sounds less in control. No one was ever hysterical in a low voice! Similarly in poetry: understatement often sounds more authoritative than high-octane, passionate exposition. However, it would be a mistake to think this meant that one is *better* than the other, though some critics – and poets – do make that error. For example, poets who rely on understatement often worry that other approaches threaten a kind of Pandora's Box of psychic and literary effects, hard to rein back in. In other words, they believe in the authority and wisdom of their own approach.

121

'Lowering your voice' is, therefore, one poetic strategy. Like speaking quietly, it creates its power by making its audience *lean in to hear it*. When we read a quiet, subtle poem, we have to concentrate to make sure we haven't missed some important detail. We can read a Sylvia Plath poem, on the other hand, with half an ear – and still understand its intention.

This is, of course, what she meant us to do. 'Writing loud' is *also* a poetic strategy, and one that's particularly relevant for women's writing. The sense, in recent culture if not still today, that a woman might have to 'shout twice as loud' to be heard means that pioneering women writers, who created textual identities where little or nothing already existed, have often resorted to a register close to overstatement in order to be 'heard' – and also to signpost the difficulty, the effort, entailed. For example, it would be easy to make an argument that the profound abjection in Simone Weil's writings, the way women like Leonora Carrington thrived in surrealism, and the note of rapture in the writings of medieval women mystics such as Julian of Norwich and Hildegard of Bingen, are all examples of a *poetics of overstatement*. Each *adopted* this technical strategy, rather than inadvertently manifesting psychological symptoms.

Whatever the particular usefulness to women poets of writing in a high register, many male poets have also elected to do so: from Modernists like T.S. Eliot and Ezra Pound, with their use of public symbols from Church and State, to the Caribbean master Derek Walcott, who earned his Nobel Prize for work that used the diction and Classical myth of his colonial education to solemnize rural experience – and was often criticized for doing so. Register, like rhyme, often has to do with cultural context. In fact, it can be culture-specific. Contemporary poetry from the Balkans is frequently dramatic, packed with symbols and abstractions, and sounds uninflected to the English ear. But when it takes its place among the contemporary design, film and even street-life of those cultures, its high colour and lack of hesitation is of a piece with what surrounds it. This is as true of the extraordinary group of middle-generation Romanian poets, including Mircea Cartarescu, Liliana Ursu and Ana Blandiana, as it is of the late great poets of the then-Yugoslavian Banat, Vasko Popa and Ivan Lalić, or younger Bulgarians Georgi Gospodinov and Tsvetaeva Elenkova. Balkan poetry also has much more of a continuing history than British poetry does as a *public* art form, with a wide mainstream audience. To take another example, Nigerian poetry is currently much more overtly political and didactic than work the Anglo-American ear is familiar with. Poets like Odia Ofeimun articulate national and local politics that are occurring within a culture of political *meetings* and *oral* democracy, and are writing for large live audiences as well as for the page. Swedish poetry of the late twentieth and early twenty-first century, on the other hand, is characteristically quiet in diction, imagery and in the claims it makes. The poems of Tomas Tranströmer and Arne Johnsson are good examples.

Choice of register, then, can be a reaction to personal or cultural context, but it can also be intrinsic to a particular poem. For example, I tend to write collections that are variegated by two contrasting textures or forms. Though all the book's poems may be related to one another, in particular thematically, the register of these two forms may differ. There may be shorter, more formal pieces – or longer, apparently loose and demotic, poems. Discursive poems may tend to a characteristically up-beat ending. Sonnets may be almost detached and questioning. And so on.

The range of possible poetic registers is excitingly large, from the oreate diction of Geoffrey Hill:

A Psalm of Reifying for the Feast
of Distances. Yuletide hazard lights
are still up:

(*The Orchards of Syon XXIX*)

to the apparently quotidian in a Neil Rollinson poem:

123

Desperate for this girl
from fifth form,
for the touch of her body,
I stand in the garden
beside her

('Hubris')

Every register, though, needs to gain the reader's assent. This 'reader of register' is the disinterested contemporary poetry reader, an individual who is responsive enough to take the work on its own terms: if not the Ideal Reader, then not the kind of 'smart-alec' critic who finds something contemptuous to say about even the most important work, either. For register can go horribly wrong when it's mismatched. When it fails, it's nearly always out of step with either context (sententiousness that feels old-fashioned and stuffy); content (that elegy for a pet hamster in heroic couplets); or deployment (you haven't handled it well and the mask slips halfway through the poem).

These mismatches produce such damaged offspring as the work of William McGonagall. With his knack for crashing bathos, McGonagall simply couldn't match the high tone he set himself:

The time is not far distant when I earnestly trust
Women will have the Parliamentary vote
And many of them, I hope, will wear a better petticoat.

(From a broadsheet)

Whereas a Scottish poet of another kind, Kathleen Jamie, uses register with coy cunning. Here she is, ironizing formal diction with the lightest of touches:

Have you not seen us, the Bairns of Suzie
under the pylons of Ormiston Brae

('Bairns of Suzie: a hex')

Wendy Cope is another mistress of register. In *Making Cocoa with Kingsley Amis*, she burst on the literary scene with a series of brilliant parodies and homages. Their irony works so well because of her ability to make allusion, conclusion and register interplay. Her poems never have the 'stickiness' of an exercise, but instead are concise, disciplined, elegant. In fact, Cope is a great example of the importance of *consistency*. She maintains her tone throughout; there are no clumsy lapses into sentimentality or sudden lurches into high-flown metaphysics.

Being in control of register is, of course, a matter of technique and therefore of practice. There are several ways to work on it. The first, and most basic, ability you need is to be able to 'catch on to' yourself using register, and the *ways* you do so. Read through three or four of your finished poems, and mark up the registers you think they use, section by section. You could give these names – *churchy, cheeky, cool* – or 'questionnaire' codes, say from H1 (very high, almost purple) through H3 and L3 to L1 (very low: demotic). If you're a synaesthete you might feel more comfortable naming colours that characterize these registers ('The Charge of the Light Brigade', being pretty high-register, might come out as imperial purple, for instance). Now do the same with three or four poems you feel aren't working, or which you gave up on. Compare the two sets of diagnoses: what do you notice? Are there any patterns, as far as you can see? For example, do your successful poems stick more closely to one or two registers throughout? Maybe they use a balanced pair of registers that alternate like dialogue? Are the unsuccessful poems a chaos of registers – or simply lopsided? Do they tend to thump into bathos? Or do they meander off prematurely into either the high-flown or the formlessly informal? Is there a correlation, do you think, between any loss of the *tonal* agenda in a poem and its stuckness?

Poems often have what the Australian poet John Kinsella calls a 'pre-cognitive' form. They are present as a kind of *pre*-shape and *pre*-tone which press at the gates of consciousness before you've consciously worked anything out. This isn't to say that poems arrive ready-formed, but they do often have *internal necessity* of form and tone. So, how do we achieve that imagined or intuited tone? Well, the writer has to *inhabit* that register as if they were an actor taking up the requisite posture for delivering a speech in a particular manner. 'Inhabiting' is, in other words, a little like method acting. It requires the writer to *enter* the register they have *selected* for their piece. They have to be wholehearted in their adherence to that register, while they're using it. It's no good trying to be both tender and cool, or improvised and formal. Two tones together are likely to crowd each other out.

This means that we need to practise a range of registers – rather than finding one that seems to work and sticking to it – in order to be able to write the poems that we could. A good – and fun – way to become adept at tone is to take existing poems by other poets and rewrite them, changing the register. A high-register poem can be 'de-consecrated' by using more demotic vocabulary and even imagery. The diction may need to shift to a more chatty style; often, word-order has to change. Meanwhile, discursive free-verse could maybe be 'talked up' by the addition of such formalities as rhyme. Until you're confident that you can hear register straightaway, on sight-reading, it's also worthwhile 'parsing the register' (in the same way as you did in your own poems) of other poets' work. This is also an interesting way to find out whether poets you admire use register in similar ways. Tonal register is one of the deep-level markers of a poem's identity and intent. It functions at an almost-unconscious, pre-cognitive level, a bit like body language.

I've left the most tricky exercise, which seems to require you to unpick your own work, till last. First you need to write a poem in high or low register: not an exercise poem, but a true poem that elects its own register. It will be the next true poem you write, in other words. Work on it, redraft it, finish it. A few days later, rewrite it in the opposite register. Again, you need to push yourself, like a method actor, to inhabit that register authentically and fully. This, too, should be as far from an exercise piece as you can get it. Leave both poems for a few days; when you return to them, ask yourself how they compare. Is one recognizably more 'yours' than the other? Do they seem like versions of the same poem – or have they become very different poems with a theme, or starting point, in common?

Register starts off sounding like a cash-book and ends up being a struggle for the very soul of a poem. And it's here, almost hidden away by being incorporated throughout its fabric, that much of the poem's power lies.

13 The uses of repetition: villanelle and ghazal

Nagging is the repetition of unpalatable truths.
Edith Summerskill (to Married Women's Association, House
of Commons, 1960)

When I teach the villanelle, I often joke that you can tell it's a form of love-poetry because of the way it uses repetition: as if to suggest obsession. However, another form that relies heavily on repetition is the ghazal (pronounced, roughly, *guzzle*). Not a romance form, it too is widely used in teaching poetry. Both of these allow the writer to deploy building-blocks of repeated material, almost like a short-cut to a completed poem. That's particularly useful for anyone new to strict verse.

But both these ancient, beautiful poetics matter for many more reasons than simply how fun they are to write. Both come from sophisticated, intensely formal traditions, in which poetic beauty is not accidental but a highly organized technical and aesthetic feat. The villanelle and the ghazal arose in cultures that prized form, ceremony, and the aesthetic order these combine to produce, as an almost moral obligation: the equivalent, perhaps, of good manners. The villanelle is a medieval French form. The customs and symbols of Courtly Love – and their corollary in action, the chivalric code – found dignity and resonance in the interplay of a small number of constrained gestures, worked over, interwoven and *gaining* in resonance through their repetition from court to court and courtship to courtship. As in the ghazal, the villanelle's inter-weaving of repeated lines, and rhymes both with and 'against' those lines, remind one of a woven tapestry. They create some-thing hieratic and static. A preponderance of repetition stops the poem moving forward in the conventional way and produces tableaux, rather than drama.

The ghazal celebrates this static, and decorative rather than emotive, character by the ultimate in self-referentiality: the poet signs himself or herself into the poem's last line. The form is composed in couplets, each repeating a single half-line, which produces a stately criss-cross of pairings in which that repeated phrase meets a series of others and moves on – as in a formal dance. Even older than the villanelle, and orig-inating in Iran as early as the seventh century, according to some sources, the ghazal's Golden Age in Persian, from the eleventh to the fifteenth centuries, produced the masters Hafez (1325–98) and Rumi (1207–73). Moghuls brought the form to India in the twelfth century, and its long tradition in Hindi and Urdu includes the work of Urdu master Ghalib (1797–1869).

Yet it's important to overcome any sense of distance this antiquity could set up. To write a successful ghazal or villanelle is to go so deeply into the form that you discover its sensibility. As we'll see again, when the next chapter looks at the sonnet, a particular *approach* to the material – even a certain range or timbre of idea – is as much part of these forms as rhyme-structure and metrical scheme. It's this atmospheric or approach that keeps the line of verse supple and living. Although strict form seems to supply many of the alternatives a poet needs to choose between, it comes alive as *true* poetry perhaps more rarely than free (or freer) verse because the temptation to let the form write the poem is so strong. We need real confidence to refuse to let the poem run on auto-matic pilot, and to question every opportunity and choice, as we do when there's no predetermined structure.

Strict form also requires real fluency with rhyme, to the point where we can be sure that we've explored every possibility at each juncture, or indeed can even play with it. Repetition intensifies the usual effects of rhyme. Think of the claustrophobia you feel in a room with patterned carpets, wallpaper, curtains *and* upholstery. But now visualize something just as ornate, but that is perfectly judged: the Moorish tiles of patios in southern Spain; Kelim wall-hangings in Albania; the West Front of Wells Cathedral. In each of these examples, repetition is used to unify *and* to structure variation. Repetition in verse also provides a unifying structure and at the same time a foundation on which to build variation. Used well, it becomes intrinsic not only to the poem's diction but to its meaning, so that it seems as natural as any other emphasis. It *makes sense* in that it underlines, or insists on, a point. And it naturalizes, because it familiarizes us with, what the poem has to say: just as the refrain in a folk song, ballad or nursery-rhyme does. This is one of the key achievements of repetition, and is the way it *unites* a poem's diction and sense.

To find out how, we need to look a little more closely at repetitive forms, starting with the villanelle. It's striking that two of the best-known villanelles in the canon of twentieth-century poetry in English are poems of loss. In Dylan Thomas's lament for his father, 'Do Not Go Gentle into that Good Night', and Elizabeth Bishop's 'One Art', written as if at the end of a relationship, the villanelle's identity as love-poem manifests as grief for a loved one. In fact, it's the villanelle's (prior) identity as love-poetry that reminds us that these laments *are* poems of love. In choosing the form, with its obsessive circling so characteristic of grief, both poets remind us how the other side of loss, indeed what predicates it, is love.

One of these famous villanelles, Bishop's 'One Art', is in fact in stricter form than the other. Thomas plays slightly loose. Both poems are in copyright, so I won't reproduce them here, but I suggest that you go and read them: they're widely available. When you do, you'll find that each is a struggle for a couplet to come together, enacting – for all the world as if Mills and Boon were straight out of the Troubadour tradition – the conventional trials of love. These two lines, which are first stated as the 'outsides' of the opening tercet – with their counterpointed middle line, which sets up a new rhyme that all the following middle lines obey – chase each other through the poem, alternating as the third line of each stanza: till they meet in the last verse, where they stand together and make direct, consecutive sense for the first time. The first line of each stanza also rhymes with this powerful couplet, creating a homogenous sound-scape that enacts the way the two lines of the couplet, like courting lovers, refer to and resonate with each other – in a cross-hatching of allusion – all through the poem.

The secret to a fine villanelle, one that sustains interest and ranges far despite this formal constriction, therefore lies in its choice of couplet. That needs both a *rhyme* straightforward enough to generate broad possibilities for development, and a *concept* strong enough to bear repetition – yet roomy enough to allow for exploration and variation, too. The easiest way to find such a couplet is to start with a strong first line. 'Do not go gentle into that good night' and 'The art of losing isn't hard to master' are both striking, memorable phrases, whether or not a poem follows. One is a command: the other is a quasi-proverbial statement. Both seem clear, yet are ambiguous. Is 'that good night' someone *saying* 'Good night' – a farewell? Or is it that 'reward' of which 'rest and sleep' are, in John Donne's sonnet 'Death Be Not Proud', mere pictures? Is the art of losing the bungle that comes all too easily to us, or an elective divesting, an aestheticism? Each opening line is underlined and answered by the second part of the couplet. 'Rage, rage against the dying of the light' offers an answering and alternative tone which makes the mood of Thomas's poem alternate between acceptance and fury. 'Disaster', and the various approaches that compose it in Bishop's villanelle, is also a deepening and darkening of register. And the 'no disaster' of the poem up to the penultimate verse is itself *turned* by the poem's last line: 'Though it may look like – *write it* – like disaster.' One of these couplets uses a feminine rhyme, the other a masculine. Both come at the end of otherwise iambic pentameter lines.

Once you've found a strong couplet, which successfully evokes a topic you want to explore, it's not a bad idea – especially for your first attempt – to sketch out the villanelle plan so you don't get lost. If **A1** and **A2** are the two lines of the couplet, and **a** all the other lines that rhyme with that couplet, then **b** are all the lines that rhyme with the poem's second rhyme, thus:

A1
b
A2

a
b
A1

a
b
A2

a
b
A1

a
b
A2

a
b
A1
A2

As this template demonstrates, neither Bishop nor Thomas is *strictly* accurate; such flexibility in a form, like flexibility in strict rhyme or metre, is the mark of a kind of mastery that comes only *after* strict formal attempts.

For practice purposes, it's a good idea to fill in the couplet lines first. They give you a sense of destination. The first line of each stanza is going to end up being answered by **A1** or **A2**, so it needs to move in that direction, while getting taken further by its second line. Mapping out these lines also allows you to see the villanelle's biggest problem. How is it possible to make each stanza, or the succession of them, bloom outwards from this strict spine: creating the curve and fullness of a poem that is all one single developing line of thought, rather than a set of variations? Try and make each stanza go somewhere further with the original idea you expressed in your couplet. You can do this by exploring a set of alternatives, as Thomas's do, or by making them into steps in one single crescendo of emphasis, like Bishop's.

Despite their strict forms, in the final stages of composition the villanelle and ghazal are like any other poem. They can be improved tremendously by small tricks of rearrangement (does this line really need to be so grammatically contorted to get us to the rhyme?), verbal adjustment (replacing full with slant rhyme, for example), rethinking of register (is that stanza really proverbial or just sententious?) and turn of phrase. It's often at this stage that the strictest forms first come to life. For proof of this, have a look at the sixteen drafts of Bishop's 'One Art' reproduced in *Edgar Allen Poe and the Juke-Box*, a collection of her drafts and juvenilia (ed. Alice Quinn, Carcanet 2007).

The ghazal is highly fashionable, and has been adopted with enthusiasm by workshop tutors. But, like the villanelle, it can be rigid and lifeless in the wrong hands. In addition, it's a form with deep roots in non-Anglophone languages and cultures, whereas Romance forms became part of the English language tradition through the ballad, medieval carol and later in Chaucerian literary poetry. The villanelle has already spent centuries as an English-language form, but to write a ghazal in English is to venture into a cross-cultural, interdisciplinary act. That fact should never be ignored since to do so is not only ignorantly appropriative, but also liable to produce limp pastiche. On the contrary, this is both an exciting and a demanding form. Even for poets with a cross-cultural background of their own, yoking together two widely differing traditions in one poem remains a challenge.

Britain's finest contemporary ghazal poet is Mimi Khalvati, born in Iran but educated in the UK from the age of six. Her *The Meanest Flower* is a deft example of this complex yoking. The book's title-sequence references Wordsworth, but does so using imagery from Khalvati's early childhood in Persia. It is also full of ghazals that combine the flexible line of the traditional form with scenes from her English life, as in her 'Ghazal: after Hafez'. The opening juxtaposes the Iranian vine and rose with the Southern English 'chine':

However large earth's garden, mine's enough,
One rose and the shade of a vine's enough.

I don't want more wealth, I don't need more lies.
In the dregs of a glass, truth shines enough.

What else can Paradise offer us beggars
And fools? What ecstasy, when wine's enough?

Come and sit by the stream. Rivers run dry
But to carry their song, a chine's enough.

The atmosphere of these lines is characteristic. 'Ghazal' is said to mean, variously, 'the cry of a captured gazelle', 'love talk', and 'talking to women'. It developed from the *tashbib*, which was in turn part of a longer form, the panegyric *qasida* – which explains the form's praise-song characteristics, including its tendency to list rather than make any tighter associations between the couplets. There are usually between five and fifteen couplets (*sher*), though the favoured number is seven, thus creating a superficial resemblance to the sonnet. The second line of each couplet ends with a repetition of the refrain (*radif*) – one or a set of words – which is immediately preceded by a word that rhymes with those in the same position in all the other couplets (*qafia*). The exception is the first couplet (*matla*), which uses this refrain and rhyme in *both* lines. The last couplet (*makhta*), though keeping to the form in every other way, is also the poem's signature, in which the poet refers to his or her own name; perhaps in the second or third person and often through metaphor. Throughout, the ghazal's *bezer*, or metre, is strict. English doesn't reproduce the nineteen Persian forms, but syllabics, iambic pentameter or other strict metre can be used.

Finally, the couplets in a ghazal can't be enjambed. Each must be able to stand alone, musically and semantically, though their relationship to each other isn't arbitrary but associative. A ghazal can sound longing and lingering, its repetitions working like a series of echoes. If that's partly because today the ghazal resounds with antiquity, it remains the best way to approach the form. The best place to start, in practising writing ghazals, is with those roots in panegyric. Think of a mood, place, atmosphere or some aspect of someone you'd like to evoke. What refrain best captures your subject? Don't make your first ghazals too long (the fourteen-line form is ideal). Start by thinking of them as listing sets of qualities. You will quickly see how such a 'list' is in fact full of interrelations. Not only is the whole more than the sum of its parts – you build up a picture – but succeeding couplets may refer to each other in various ways. They can escalate, or move through the senses, for example. Nevertheless, restraint, both in directly *articulating* these connections and in expressing how you *feel* about your subject, is part of the character of a true ghazal. The sensibility that the form allows you to discover should be almost the opposite of the single-pointed *ego* of the Western Romantic tradition. The ghazal celebrates the world around it, but *not* its own speaker. A useful way to remember this is to tell yourself that's why the poet's *name* is formally celebrated at the end of the poem. It's the public persona, your name and your poetic skill, rather than the inner life of what you think and feel, that the poem records.

Because they're both formal and yet accessible to the general reader, the villanelle and ghazal remind us of one of the most important arts of poem-making. They are unashamedly concerned with *making something beautiful*: with art. That art may be an end in itself in a ghazal in a way that differs from the more overtly expressive villanelle form. But, in its traditional relationship with the non-literary reader, it reminds us what poetry could be for.

14 The sonnet: working it out

And sweet as are her lips that speak it, she
Now learns the tongues of France and Italy
Andrew Marvell, 'To his Worthy Friend Doctor Witty upon
his Translation of the Popular Errors'

It's no coincidence that the term 'sonnet' includes the word 'song', nor is it a coincidence that we hear a diminutive *ette* at the end of it. A sonnet is a *little song*: which is first of all to say that it's *public*, as a song is. A song isn't just a line of (poetic) thought; it's something that is done *out loud*. Who knows what birds are thinking? Their song, though, is uttered. The sonnet is by nature 'done aloud' because it's a love form. It has an addressee: not just an Ideal Reader, that sophisticated construct of literary work, but an individual whose role is to be not a mere part of the poetic process, but its goal.

Like the villanelle, the sonnet is a form that derives from medieval Europe, with its low levels of literacy even among the aristocracy (in women, for example); so its formal roots are partly performative – and include literal singing. Petrarch developed the sonnet in the fourteenth century, in his *Canzione* for Laura. Early examples of the sonnet in English were written by Thomas Wyatt, among others, at the start of the sixteenth century. As this historical tradition shows, the

137

sonnet is a cultural construct – an artefact – at the same time as having an individual addressee.

We'll look more closely at the sonnet's formal requirements in a moment. However, its link with song also means that the form's public utterance is melodic. Not surprisingly, this entails scansion and rhyme, with the chime of regular form. But it also reminds us that *song* in English-language poetry always refers, at least in part, to the lyric tradition – one that has to do with content as well as form. The sonnet is member par excellence of the lyric tradition, which is in essence individual. Only an individual can be in love, even if poets as varied as John Donne and Gerard Manley Hopkins have written poems whose narrator is in love with God. William Wordsworth's 'On Westminster Bridge' is a love-poem to a city. Nevertheless, though he might love a collective, such as a nation or family, it is the individual's experience that the sonnet captures. The lyric poem expresses an individual viewpoint and experience, and associates these with, or tries to make of them, some form of beauty. As its name also suggests, a sonnet 'picks up' experience and sets it ringing. A sour-toned sonnet doesn't work – though it's perfectly possible to write fourteen lines of fine satirical verse, for example.

But that diminutive suffix also modifies the sonnet's implied lyric ease: the suggestion of the spontaneous and straightforward that the idea of 'song', and the form's use of the first person, bring to it. This little song is not narratively extended like the ballad, nor extended through repetition like the villanelle or sestina. The sonnet is the clenched fist of the lyric tradition. It's where nothing is spun out or delayed. On the contrary, everything is condensed. As we'll see, sonnets are complex with *simultaneity*, and that entails both condensation and acceleration. If you have two things happening at once, rather than one after the other, they pull on each other like warp and weft, making a dense, interesting texture. They're rather removed, in fact, from the single line of a melody. Indeed, we could say that the sonnet is the form that introduces counterpoint to English verse. It is also the apotheosis of the courtly Romance tradition, in which language, and the ideas it carries, become intricately wrought and clearly removed from the anonymous, oral forms of folk traditions.

Let's look at a couple of famous sonnets:

On first looking into Chapman's Homer

Much have I travell'd in the realms of gold,
 And many goodly states and kingdoms seen;
 Round many western islands have I been
Which bards in fealty to Apollo hold.
Oft of one wide expanse had I been told
 That deep-brow'd Homer ruled as his demesne;
 Yet did I never breathe its pure serene
Till I heard Chapman speak out loud and bold:
Then felt I like some watcher of the skies
 When a new planet swims into his ken;
Or like stout Cortez when with eagle eyes
 He star'd at the Pacific—and all his men
Look'd at each other with a wild surmise—
 Silent, upon a peak in Darien.

(John Keats)

And:

On His Blindness

When I consider how my light is spent
 E're half my days, in this dark world and wide,
 And that one Talent which is death to hide,
 Lodg'd with me useless, though my Soul more bent
To serve therewith my Maker, and present
 My true account, lest He returning chide,
 Doth God exact day-labour, light deny'd?
 I fondly ask: But Patience to prevent
That murmur, soon replies: God doth not need

Either man's work, or his own gifts, who best
 Bear his milde yoak, they serve him best, his State
Is Kingly. Thousands at his bidding speed
And post o'er Land and Ocean without rest:
They also serve who only stand and waite.

(John Milton)

It's easy to see from these examples that a sonnet has four-teen lines. You can also observe that these lines rhyme, though not always to the same pattern, and are regular in length. The conventional sonnet is written in the familiar iambic pentame-ter. As we saw in Chapter 4, an iamb allows the line to land on a masculine ending, which is usually seen as more satisfactory for English rhyming. You only have to rhyme the last syllable, and it's more likely to be a full rhyme. A feminine ending has to rhyme a *trajectory*, the *relationship* between the last strong syllable and the weaker one following it. This makes it much more likely that assonance, or slant rhyme, will be the 'best' you can do. Thus, *weather* can find itself 'rhymed' with both *water* and *other* as well as with the more predictable *blether* or *endeavour*. The sonnet's strict form has traditionally eschewed such experiments. Even today, to use slant rhyme in a sonnet is to court the possibility that your poem will be described as 'sonnet-*like*' or 'fourteen-lined'.

Probably because of its relationship with the iamb, pentameter remains the norm, though the quatrameter or hexameter sonnet is more prevalent than one that is slant rhymed. However, all sonnets balance their weight in a char-acteristic way, around an approximation to the Golden Section. The sonnet divides into two parts: the first eight lines (the octet) and final six (the sestet). These can be marked out by rhyme-schemes (of which more in a moment), but will always be distinguished by a change in the sonnet's direction of thought: this is known as *the turn*. The first eight lines are, in effect, the sonnet's *sortie* – it goes out and establishes its ground and themes. It characterizes itself: this is a sonnet in which the love-object is God, or the city of London. Its atmosphere may be regretful, optimistic or horny. A particular set of images is developed. Then – since fourteen lines are not very many – by line nine it already needs to begin to make its way home, transformed in some way, but surefooted and aiming for resolution.

Musicians call endings *cadences*. These are where what the ear's been expecting happens, and everything is resolved at last in two or three final chords. *Interrupted* and *imperfect* cadences swivel music into something new, rather like the sonnet turn, but the form's closing couplet, which is among the most powerful arrivals at certainty to be found in literature, operates like a *perfect* cadence, underlining arrival and closure with full rhyme.

Another way to think about the *turn* on which the proportions of the sonnet hinge is that the first eight lines are speculation, the next six accumulation. I prefer thinking in terms of exposition and resolution. But a sonnet doesn't operate like a simple question and answer. The material of the first part *is resolved* in the second: and that's a *process* in verse. Usually, this process means resolving two simultaneous tracks in a sonnet's thought. Just as a villanelle stages the laborious, eventual, coming-together of the two lines of its couplet – as if to mimic the processes of lovers – so the sonnet stages the resolution, or coming together, of two strands. These are often two sides of a metaphor, a paradox, or even of register. Because they generate the poem's tension, they must be resolved in order for it to come to rest. In Shakespeare's famous sonnet 'Shall I compare thee to a Summer's Day?', the 'compare' is an extended metaphor declaring itself. The poem does indeed compare the loved one to a summer day. In the process, aspects of this simile (as it in fact is) are explored and exhausted. It turns out that the girl wins out because her beauties won't fade – because of this poem, which immortalizes them. This elegant piece of rhetoric doubles its own terms in *both* directions. The simile of the summer day is in turn metaphorized in terms of loans; the girl's virtues outstrip summertime's to the extent that her lover's outstrip hers (it is *he* who has the gift of immortality – which he *loans* her):

> So long as lips can read and eyes can see
> So long lives this, and this gives life to thee.

The sustained conceit in William Wordsworth's 'On Westminster Bridge' is just as sophisticated. The poem starts by accusing the passer-by who can ignore the view from Westminster Bridge of having a 'dull . . . soul' or, as we might say, sleep-walking. The poem transfers an intimation of life to the not-yet-woken, not-yet-workaday city: yet keeps London asleep too, so that the whole poem seems like a dream. In the end, we're not sure who dreamt it – poet or city.

Paradox is even closer than extended metaphor to the heart of the sonnet, not only because it's more susceptible to *development*, but because the sonnet, by associating love with having things to work out, is committed to an idea about the paradoxical nature of love itself. In the sonnet, to express love is always somehow to *long*: the form expresses the *aporia* between lover and love-object as well as expressing love itself. No wonder it's often used, by poets from John Donne to Herbert Lomas, to address a God – surely the most complex and ambiguous of human loves, and certainly one with a strong sense of distance built into it! – as well as other non-romantic loves, such as patriotism or love of landscape. Christian iconography – the tradition within which the sonnet form evolved – is an especially fine resource for poetic paradox, as it expresses fear, anguish and loneliness in terms of love; and uses the terms of sexual desire to articulate sacred emotions. For the reader, too, this kind of ambiguity is what makes the poem interesting. No one wants to read about stasis: there's no hook, and nothing goes on in the reading. Just as romantic fiction has to create difficulty before it offers resolution, so paradox or distance within love is what leaves the poet something to say.

Rhyme-schemes underline the work the sonnet undertakes. Generally, the octet rhymes with itself and the sestet starts a new set of rhymes. The sestet does not have to close with a rhyming couplet – the last line can rhyme with lines 13, 12, 11 or 9 – though, if it does so, it allows a tone of particular finality: the difference between that Shakespeare and the Milton and Keats examples. So it's good to embark on the sestet with a sense of whether or not you want a Grand Finale, rather than allowing the rhyme-scheme to emerge by happenstance. Sonnets can be written in stanzas – often three quatrains and a couplet, like Don Paterson's *Sonnets to Orpheus* – and even in couplets: as is the whole of the verse novel *For All We Know*, by Ciaran Carson. The hardest scheme for a sonnet is, arguably, rhyming couplets. Their local pull would make it hard to build the aural and semantic arch that carries a thought throughout a poem, allowing the sonnet to *work through* its concerns.

The most famous forms are the Petrarchian, or Italian, and the Shakespearean, or English, sonnets. Petrarch's form consists of an octave rhyming *abba abba* and a sestet, usually rhyming *cde cde*, although *ccd ccd* is common too. What this form doesn't do is land on a final rhyming couplet. In the sixteenth century, the English sonnet form emerged, developed by the Earl of Surrey, Shakespeare and others – perhaps helped by the fact that sonnets had become highly fashionable. The English sonnet consisted of three quatrains and a final couplet, which Shakespeare rhymed *abab cdcd efef gg*. By the end of the century the sonnet sequence, often of more than a hundred poems, had been developed as a love form, not only by Shakespeare but by Sir Philip Sidney (*Astrophil and Stella*) and Edmund Spenser (*Amoretti*). In imitation of Petrarch, these sequences addressed a single ideal woman or muse. Finally, Spenser's *Amoretti* kept the closing couplet of the English form, but locked the quatrains together with interwoven rhyme: *abab bcbc cdcd ee*. However, Milton and his successors, especially the Romantic poets, returned to variations on the Petrarchian form.

The rules about rhyme-schemes have become increasingly flexible. A contemporary sonnet can rhyme: *abca dcbd effe gg*.

Such more dispersed or hidden rhymes serve to 'quieten' the form, while keeping the density of sonnet structure. Petrarchian and Shakespearean forms share the formal marker of the 'turn' between octet and sestet, but the Spenserian sequence starts to collapse these precise proportions. Although it distinguishes the start of the final sestet in the rhyme-scheme, it does so via a repetition. This reminds us that the other side of a thematic 'turn' is consistency: material is turned *within* the sonnet. Rhyme-schemes that soften the move into the last six lines take this further still, allowing us to think instead of a *proportionate pull* between two aspects of material taking place throughout the sonnet.

The sonnet is a lively contemporary form. In particular, it's worth looking at further examples by Jo Shapcott (who translates Rilke, as Paterson does), Tony Harrison (iambic pentameter's most persuasive adept), and Seamus Heaney, whose 'Glanmore Sonnets' are full of cheeky slant rhyme. As you do so, you'll notice how greatly the sonnet differs from the villanelle and the ghazal. Not even diction, let alone formal choice, remains characteristic from poet to poet.

So how to make a start on a sonnet of your own? This comes down to how you'd normally start a poem. While some poets compose line by perfect line, others throw down a first draft to sketch out what they've got to say. It's all down to you. Nevertheless, with strict form, a first line is generally the best starting point: a phrase that has in it something which intrigues you, and that has formed itself clearly in your mind. At this stage, don't worry too much what that line seems to be about. A landscape or streetscape can turn into a profession of love, or longing, for a place – or someone associated with it. Even a still life can be praised. The *mood* of what you have to say does matter, though. You have to *be in a relationship* to what you're writing about; whether you address it, or simply describe it in intimate, connected terms. Objectivity and alienation produce fourteen-line poems, not sonnets. On the other hand, *struggling* with an understanding – something that, arguably, goes on within most relationships as well as the experience of reading – *can* produce a sonnet.

As with much formal verse, it's good to let your second line and the approach to the third grow naturally out of the first if you can. After all, it's only as you come into the third line that you need to start to worry about which rhyme-scheme you're going to use. Check the possibilities: does one have a particularly instinctive appeal, perhaps because it seems transparent (*abab*) or criss-crosses self-referentially (*abacdcdb*)? If not, prepare to be guided, at this stage, simply by whether or not you can make a good rhyme that moves the poem on. Begin to bear in mind that you've eight lines in which to state your case, and you're already on the third. It could be a good idea to put dots down the margin marking out the remaining extent of the octet: just to give yourself a sense of how far you have to go.

The sonnet is one of the most intimate, as well as the densest, of love forms: the one most epistolary or vocative in character. It's a good idea to imagine yourself *speaking* your emerging poem. Imagine you're using an intimate, informal voice to address someone sitting close to you. This should help you counteract the grandstanding tendencies of strict form. It also keeps your eye on what the sonnet intrinsically is. Tone is often what emerging poets find most difficult, since its necessity comes from this *address*: from whom it speaks to, and how.

Although the sonnet isn't collective, or polemic, or aggrandizing, it *may* be witty, sly, affectionate, passionate – or argumentative. It's always one supple line of thought. And suppleness requires regular exercise. In order to keep the sonnet you are drafting as supple as possible, keep thinking ahead with part of your mind while concentrating on the line in hand with the other. It's like driving: looking through the windscreen, you also glance in the driving mirror and know what's behind you as if doing both at the same time. In particular, as you embark on the sestet, bear the closure of the last line or couplet in mind. Meanwhile, the turn itself needs to be marked by content, not a lurch in form. Indeed – as with enjambment more generally – the more fluid the formal demarcation of the turn, the more fluent it feels. Too radical a shift – just like moving in or out of form altogether – reads like technical failure, not poetic choice. The sestet shouldn't have a rhyme-scheme that moves too far away from that of the octet. For example, it's not a good idea to start suddenly rhyming in couplets.

Some poets avoid the close-down of a final full rhyme. Their reasons for doing so are poetic, and may indicate subtlety of register, or a kind of open-endedness in which the poem refuses to 'resolve' itself after all. Jacob Polley's sonnets, in *Little Gods*, often dispense with even the final full stop. However, this is the kind of decision that a sonnet needs to engender at least as far back as the turn: maybe even from the outset. If it has been tight-knit until ending abruptly, you need to check whether it has 'earned' that openness.

Now that you've finished the first draft of your sonnet, ask yourself a key question. *Is it memorizable?* Writing of this length, and in strict form, should be if it's to be at all memorable. If it's not, what's wrong with your poem? Try saying it aloud: where do you get stuck? Is it at a point which, now you look closely, is rather out of focus, either rhythmically or in what it says? Something must be keeping the reader out. Has your sonnet got too discursive and dry? Isn't it singing enough? These aren't formal questions, but general poetic ones, which don't go away, whether you write experimental, traditional formal or free-verse. Often, when a poet first works in a particular form, they become absorbed by its 'crossword' aspect, and forget about the living line. The sonnet's very name reminds you to keep that line singing.

15 Re-solving problems: redrafting and translation

Why Bottom, thou art translated.
> William Shakespeare, *A Midsummer Night's Dream*

A friend of mine says, with Edna St Vincent Millay, that Elbert Hubbard was wrong. Life isn't just one damn thing after another, it's *the same* damn thing after another. Art, ever ready to imitate life, can sometimes seem akin to housework, as we try repeatedly to make a cleaner, brighter text. The worst thing about housework is this repetition. It's bad enough painting a room. How much more tedious no sooner to have swept out the cobwebs than they reappear?

Much of writing is redrafting: a process of working on something that won't come right. We all fantasize about a single act of composition in which the poem emerges complete: as in the barn-building scene in Peter Weir's 1985 film *Witness*, where, to the accompaniment of striding post-Copland 'frontier' music, a fictional Amish community get together and build a barn in a single day. But most writing seems more like banging in crooked nails, patching up with WD-40, sanding down the door that always sticks. It's hard to learn the patience – and the confidence – to carry this process through. It is easier to believe that working on a poem is fussing: or, worse still, pretentious. It can be hard to recognize it's necessary. Analogously, I work in an office where we've all got so used to not turning on the hot tap in the washroom that we've practically forgotten that actually we *ought* to have hot water in our workplace. One of the reasons so many writers try to defamiliarize their poems during drafting – reading them aloud, or printing out later versions rather than working with them on-screen – is that once you know a poem well it's hard to see where it truly *needs* work.

Surely this suggests too much confidence, rather than too little? It can. But it can also suggest *settling* for something. When I was a child I used to wonder why everyone had such ugly floral upholstery and curtains. I knew that perfectly good, classic prints existed. I'd seen them in magazines, on TV, and even in our local department store. Of course, I now know that everyone where we lived had ugly prints because they were cheaper. They were a *gesture towards* the thing people really wanted, and you learnt to 'look through' them to imagine the attractive stuff families really intended to have. What the cheap prints did – apart from develop our imaginations – was help us to internalize the fact that we were second-class. For reasons that were beyond our control (and therefore existential), we couldn't have the real thing. That easily translates, especially to a young mind, as *not deserving* the real thing.

A lot of emerging poets seem equally happy to settle for something less than the real thing. Their poems aren't as original or perceptive as their own conversation – or their reading *of* poetry. They assume that all they can be is a second-class poet: a mirror and not a lamp to poetry, to steal M.H. Abrams's metaphor. They don't want to – or don't believe they can – write a poem that makes the scales fall from readers' eyes, shocks the system, and travels round the English-speaking world like an intellectual virus. Although they may *think* they are doing so, they draw back from 'going that extra mile' towards the truly challenging sound, emotion or thought. Even emerging poets who long to be published often shy away from the rigour and dedication with which every great poet of the past has famously applied themselves. I don't believe this is just laziness and arrogance. As Nelson Mandela said in his famous inauguration speech in 1994, it's a human fear that we either can't be, or don't deserve, the real thing:

> Our deepest fear is not that we are inadequate. Our deepest fear is that we are powerful beyond measure. It is our light, not our darkness, that most frightens us.

Of course every poem, being manmade, is imperfect. Every poem, however great, necessarily fails in its attempt to transcend the human being who made it. But poems *can* get a long way towards that goal; and they get a lot further when the intention and practice are genuinely there. Beckett's great line from his 1983 novel *Worstward Ho*, is: 'Try again. Fail again. Fail better.' Trying again can go on in the making of a single poem. I've written pieces that started out being free-verse and ended up as rhyming couplets. Some poets, bilingual like the first National Poet of Wales Gwyneth Lewis, *rewrite* their own poems in another language. Samuel Beckett did the same.

A classic exercise in writing workshops is to cut up prose, to find the 'hidden' poetic music, as the late great Raymond Carver did with short passages of translated prose by Chekhov in his last book of poetry, *A New Path to the Waterfall*. Redrafting a poem isn't necessarily so radical, but always entails *rewriting*, even if it changes only one word or a single comma. It's a form of *composition*, with all the creativity that implies, and not an exercise or a chore. If the poem is any good at all, it will be improved, not weakened, by this process. 'What doesn't kill you makes you stronger', as our grandmothers used to say. That may not be true for humans, but it certainly is for poems. Like pots, or biblical saints, they need to go through a 'refiner's fire' of radical inspection and experimentation before they can be finished.

Poets fortunate enough to have an early mentor, or to do a Creative Writing MA, learn redrafting through apprenticeship. An established professional writer will demonstrate, in word-by-word detail, where the weaknesses or problems are in their work. They'll learn, through examples from their *own* poems, the questions to ask and ways to solve problems in order to redraft effectively. Without this experience of the actual process of redrafting, it's very hard for an emerging writer to make their own process as rich as it could be. So in this chapter we're going to try a different approach, and come at redrafting by analogy.

A while ago, I was commissioned to write a poem for the Coull String Quartet. Because we performed it first as a work in progress, and a later version went on the web, they got to see the process of redrafting at first hand. We had several conversations about how similar this process feels, for me, to refining a performance. Performers 'learn' a piece, but *continue* to develop their understanding of it – and possibly even to solve technically difficult corners – through practice. You could say that the ideal performance is always already there within their knowledge of the piece: they just have to get to it. It's like the old cliché that the statue is already in the lump of marble. Redrafting – arguably, even initial composition – is something like this. The ideal poem isn't a *construct*, it's always already *in there*, in the language or thought or the world, waiting for the disfiguring bits of 'stone' (language) to be cut away so it can come clear.

Here, as an example, are three drafts of a poem I was working on last year. They differ not only in length but, as a result, in tone. They shift even their cultural resonances – from Eliot to Delius. The first version given here looks, in retrospect, like an ideas list: but it's already in a form:

The Stone Fruit Garden

Quick, quick!

1.
All summer
        you waited for summer.

The days were shocked, lightless;
grass paled, flowers bleached.
You caught that indoor look

as if your face
came from the mirror's silvered interior.

Listless afternoons. Butterflies paired
in patches of light
that seemed happenstance as rain-showers
or passing traffic –
                  the way each car approaches,
packed with narrative,
                  then fades
to a relinquishing thrum.

You were waiting for heat.
You wanted some outsize brightness
to open overhead,
                  like a sign
that the quotidian leads, after all,
to intense, incarnated happiness –

your neighbours' voices, as they dug onions,
ringing clearly through the afternoon,
skylarks ascending in spirals.
It was as if the world were unchanged, after all,
carrying you
                  forward –

One day your body would luxuriate in this,
freckling, opening
                  towards an eventual heat.
Perhaps it was very much
like being loved.

2.
for Martin Harrison

When you talk about his stone-fruit orchard,
your fourteenth-century *Coeur de boeuf*,

the space round this plastic table
where you've brought your *café crèmes* – under plane-trees –

fills with leaf-shapes, flavours.
Gooseberry, persimmon, Japanese pear,

quince, lime-trees, lavender by a back door,
brambles, fruit-flies, nectarines and plums

which, when they flower, make galaxies in his poem.
So, you can conjure beauty –

easy as stirring coffee
with this plastic eye-of-a-needle spoon –

and something's changed by such ease. Not friendship.
Maybe the way language turns plants

into shared currency,
a shortcut between two places

high on opposite sides of the globe.
The Hunter Valley. The Vale of the White Horse:

it's as if the names squint across at each other
or, rather, come forward expecting to shake on it –

Something about this coincidence
has to do with embodiment;

bark-grain and smell and the way names *place* you

in planting themselves round you.

3.
Impossible to be a gardener
and practise *haeccitas*,
surely? Here under your drenched ash
are foxglove stragglers, the button-blush
of new apples, lavender dark with minerals –

a floppy abundance.
If you tidied it,
something you find you need
would be gone, irrevocably as Cuckoo Pen's
unpredictable callers, two years on:

their absence,
tidied away,
is a lesson in absolutes.
The very opposite of these unnamed trumpets
crowding your flower-beds.

I loved the title of this draft, but I felt the poem lacked a
spine. It had too many things to say and I had to admit I prob-
ably needed more than one poem to say them. So, instead of
three views of a global garden, I looked for one single take on
the shared experience of climate change. I started with the
section that I felt was least general and vague. It was also the
passage that interested me the most because I hadn't written
before about friendship, a topic that seems much more
complex and subtle to express than love:

After Delius

When you and Martin talk about a stone-fruit orchard,
rare *Coeur de boeuf* tree-stock,

you fill the dusty café terrace near St Sulpice

with persimmon, Japanese pear, lavender in pots,
bramble, nectarines;
                  even those plums
which, when they flower,
appear as galaxies in one of his poems.

So – you can rustle these up,
easy as stirring your coffee with a plastic spoon?

That must change something.
       Not friendship
perhaps, but the way language turns plants
to currency,
making a shortcut between gardens
on opposite sides of the globe.
The Hunter Valley. Vale of the White Horse:
the names squint across at each other,
or, rather, come forward expecting to shake on this –

something to do with living in the body,
grain, scent,
the way names place you
as they plant themselves around you.

. . . All summer, waiting for summer
you're pale, as if you lived
in a mirror's silvered interior.

It's the jet-stream,
the newspaper explains
with the aid of arrows. *Expect worse to come.*

Well . . . You want an out-sized sun
to open overhead
           as a sign
of how things could work out:
your neighbours' voices

ringing again through fine afternoons,

skylarks springing
                their high spirals.

Instead, rain like tabloid arrows
soaks a lawn, crowded by roses, daisies, thyme,

where someone's laid a clutch of pebbles
on a bench under the ash –
so perhaps the grass isn't empty, as it seems,
but thronged with ghosts
strolling hand-in-hand

or sitting to face, in each other's eyes,
the end of the world.

Strange, that the New Life might end
with a garden, small measure you started from:
remember the wooden summerhouse, *leylandii*,
that robin, quick with instinct
at your feet?

              The suburban paradise
locking its gates around you,
just as you feared,
on afternoons that smell of grass and rot –
your whole life between slipping away –

and you a child again,
among light and shade, in the silent garden.

Well, this seemed better but was still rather indigestible. Perhaps I'd made the Delius allusions too central with this title. Offputting, surely, for anyone who didn't care about music. And anyway, my poem wasn't a nostalgic pastoral. It might be seeing the end of the world in a garden, but that was

in the future and hardly pastoral. I decided to break up what
I had to say into manageable chunks:

A Walk to the Paradise Garden

> *. . . loading galaxies of flowers / like night sky's sprawling fire*
>
> Martin Harrison

I

When you and Martin talk about a stone-fruit orchard,
rare *Coeur de boeuf* tree-stock,
you fill the dusty café terrace near St Sulpice
with persimmon, lavender in pots,
bramble,
      even those flowering plums
which appear as galaxies in one of his poems.

So – you can rustle these up, easy as stirring your coffee . . .
That must change something. Not friendship
perhaps, but the way language
cuts between gardens
on opposite sides of the globe –

Vale of the White Horse, Hunter Valley,
the names bring you home
as they plant themselves round you.

II

. . . All summer, waiting for summer,
you're pale, as if you lived
in a mirror's silvered interior.
It's the Jet Stream. Expect worse to come.

Well . . . You want an out-size sun
to open overhead, as a sign

of how things could work out,
your neighbours' voices
ringing through fine afternoons,
skylarks springing
                    their high spirals.

Instead, rain soaks a lawn
crowded by roses, daisies, thyme –
where someone's laid a clutch of pebbles
on a bench under the ash.
So perhaps the grass isn't empty, but thronged
with ghosts strolling hand-in-hand,
the end of the world
reflected in each other's eyes.

Strange, that the New Life might end
with a garden, provincial measure you started from

(remember the wooden summerhouse,
that robin, quick with instinct
at your feet . . .)

                    the suburban paradise
locking its gates around you
just as you feared,
on afternoons that smell of grass and rot –
the life between slipping away
and you, childish, among light and shadow
in the silent garden.

This final version meant I'd lost, for now, many of the
things I wanted to say: both ideas and images. But the one
thing the poem *did* say was much clearer. Its whole character
had changed, too, from a survey to something quite specifi-
cally located. And that in turn had shifted its diction, from the
loosely descriptive into greater clarity.

Not every poet writes in the same way: some 'transcribe'

line by line, over a period of days, and make only small adjustments in the redrafting stages. Others, like Elizabeth Bishop, produce a first draft that is more like a map or template of the potential poem. They may revise, as she sometimes did, over a period of years. I've mentioned the series of facsimiles of her villanelle 'One Art' in Alice Quinn's *Edgar Allen Poe and the Juke Box*. In his biography of Wilfred Owen, Jon Stallworthy looks at drafts of the poet's 'What passing bells . . .' It's fascinating to see famous phrases come into being step by step. What seems, retrospectively, absolutely necessary does not automatically appear so at the time. The phrase that gets held on to, marring the poem, till the penultimate draft – while the reader, like someone watching a horror film, knows better than stumbling genius *what they should write* and wants to shout at them, 'Hurry up!' or 'It's behind you!' – that phrase is probably the one the poet was most attached to. They thought it was a real triumph – it may have been one of the first lines they thought of – but it was just a growing device, a ladder to climb to the finished poem.

One of the first strategies of redrafting, then, is to put mental brackets round any phrase you think particularly fine. Another is to check you need that opening line, phrase or stanza. Writing poetry, almost as much as prose, often seems to require a warm-up, something to test the ground. Like the favourite phrase, it may have been necessary to get the poem started, but not be needed to finish it. Gwyneth Lewis reports how Joseph Brodsky used to tell his students to cut the first stanza, or paragraph, once they'd written a piece. A third strategy is to check for register. Is your poem lapidary, discursive, lyric? Does it stay that way – or does it lurch between styles and registers? If so, it hasn't yet fully resolved the question of its own identity. Fourth come specifics of meaning and grammar: the kind of problem we looked at in Chapters 9 and 10.

If you can't work with a practising writer, one of the best ways to an apprenticeship in redrafting – which is to say in writing – poetry is through literary translation. *You do not need to be any kind of linguist for this.* All you need is a good dictionary or glossary. But why bother with literary translation? Surely, in the little time you have free, you need to concentrate on your own writing? Well, literary translation *is* your own writing. That's why a poet as major as Robert Lowell published his volume of *Imitations* of great poems from the European canon. It's why the best poets writing in Britain today make versions and translations of poets from Sophocles (Ruth Fainlight, Robin Robertson) to Rilke (Don Paterson, Jo Shapcott), Yannis Ritsos (David Harsent) to Cavafy (widely attempted). And that's not to mention the many versions of Ovid, including Michael Hofmann and James Lasdun's collection of versions by well-known American and British poets, *After Ovid*, and Ted Hughes's *Tales from Ovid*, which have been enormously influential in the last twenty years.

Literary translation is your own writing because *all* the rewriting stages are yours, in exactly the same way as they are in any other poem you work on. There are constraints – the requirements of some degree of fidelity to the original – just as there are formal and other constraints in a poem you have originated. The detailed decisions, though, come down to expressing what you want to express (such as each of the steps in the poem's development of an idea, or an aspect of characterization that you find particularly important) within the limits of the language available to you in this particular context (for example, it needs to rhyme; or you need an explicatory pronoun because objects aren't gendered in English).

A great introduction to literary translation is to take a well-known poem and compare fine existing translations of it. The web is very useful for this, but so is a decent library. Look at Lorca translated by Roy Campbell, by Merryn Williams, and by the American poets collected in Christopher Mauris's edition; read Cavafy translated by Aliki Barnstone and Stratis Havinias and in the Keeley and Sherrard selection; compare versions of Celan by Ian Fairley, Michael Hamberger and in the versions edited by Pierre Joris. What you realize is that there are several ways to re-tell a poem. Some will appeal more to your own poetic taste than others. Even meaning is not stable. It's something conjured up by choices and patterns of words. Once you've read three or more translations of a poem, you find yourself developing a sense of *not like this – but like this* and wanting to 'correct' where you think a text hasn't grasped the character of the original. That kind of reactive reading is the first step into making your own translation.

Serious literary translation, intended for publication, starts with close study of the original. Most poets who publish work of this nature are not philologists, but have decided to translate poems by someone whose writing they admire. They usually do this with the help of basic English drafts and a series of detailed questions about the shades of meaning in a word. Only someone with the *combined* skills of a native speaker and a major poet (such as the original author) can answer these questions at the level necessary: the level at which the original poet was working with his or her language. In other words, such questions about nuance ought to be asked – if not of the original poet then of literary scholars – by professional translators, however exceptional their language skills, if they're going to produce anything resembling a literary text. Poets who do lots of translating themselves are particularly good at providing literal translations. At their intelligent best, these are annotated with comment on ambiguities and register, on allusion and pun; as well as supplying the sound and form of the original. Here for example is a literal prepared, with Amir Or, for his poem 'Epitaph':

Whole poem literal, 'Epitaph'

1. Turn off/ divert/ incline (horizontally) from the way of going, you the traveller,
2. Sit among trees of berry and vine.
3. Between/among water and shade and the whiteness of stone
4. Here lie I, (a) boy and (a) king.

5. My face[1] cold marble. My hands/palms, my legs/feet[2].

6. I am dressed/clothed with/in ferns and a-collective-noun-for-fallen-leaves[34].

7. Also I, (I too) didn't far-go[56],

8. Also[7] I was alive[8].

9. Turn off/ divert/ incline (horizontally) from the way of going, you the traveller[9],

10. Smash[10] wild berries[11] on/against[12] my face.

[1] No 'is' in Hebrew, but there is an alternative construction which works as 'is' that the poet has not used.

[2] There are specific terms for these body parts, but the poet has used the words with more inclusive meanings.

Repetition of sound throughout this line because of the 'my (male, plural)' suffix.

[3] Has a secondary meaning of the state of trees which are losing their leaves. Analogy in English might be with use of 'moult': what its body is doing and the moulted fur itself.

[4] Onomatopoeic alliterations – sh then ch (and at the end of the line r, l) – run through every word in the line except for 'I (ani).

[5] And the ch carries on into the next line.

[6] Hebrew verb something like s'éloigner (French). Analogy in English, about time rather than space, would be use of 'prolong' – a sense of how far that extension is. Important resonance as this is existential as well as a physical protraction.

[7] 'Also' in the same sense as line 7, of 'I too', rather than 'and another point is'.

[8] Both existence and animation.

[9] Exact repeat.

[10] Violently break apart, c.f. biblical use either by ripping (the lion rips apart the man on the road) or crushing (Babylonians crush babies on rocks). A verb representing the damage caused (to berries) by impact rather than the action leading to it.

[11] Can only be red in Hebrew: and we know the face is cold white marble, so red on white. Also violent action on mineral inertia.

[12] Not into – no penetration of face.

As with first stanza, rhyme in second stanza is c (c,c) d d c, with internal rhyme in first line (note 2). The d rhyme brings together falling leaves and going far in life. In c rhyme, being alive has to do with (living) hands, feet and face. So the rhymes in this stanza highlight agreement rather than contradiction as in first stanza.

Final couplet returns us to a *c* rhyme.

Rhythm: the first time we have only 4 feet in a line is line 8, with 'alive'. The last line is also only 3 feet.

אֶפִּיטָף	Epitaph
נְטֵה מִן הַדֶּרֶךְ, אַתָּה הַהֹלֵךְ,	neTE min haDErech, aTA ha'HElech,
שֵׁב בֵּין עֲצֵי הַתּוּת וְהַגֶּפֶן.	SEV bein aTSEY haTUT vehaGEfen.
בֵּין מַיִם וָצֵל וְלֹבֶן הָאֶבֶן	bein MAyim vaTSEL veLOven ha'Even
פֹּה שׁוֹכֵב אֲנִי, נַעַר וּמֶלֶךְ.	po shoCHEV aNI, NA'ar uMElech.
פְּנֵי שַׁיִשׁ קַר. יָדַי, רַגְלַי.	paNAY SHAyish KAR. yaDAY,
אֲנִי לָבוּשׁ בִּשְׂרָכִים וְשַׁלֶּכֶת.	ragLAY.
גַּם אֲנִי לֹא הִרְחַקְתִּי לָלֶכֶת,	ani aTUF bishraCHIM veshaLEchet.
גַּם אֲנִי הָיִיתִי חַי.	gam aNI lo hirCHAKti laLEchet,
	gam aNI haYIti CHAY.
נְטֵה מִן הַדֶּרֶךְ, אַתָּה הַהֹלֵךְ,	
רַטֵּשׁ תּוּתַי בָּר עַל פָּנַי.	neTE nin haDErech, aTA haHElech,
	raTESH tutey BAR al paNAY.
CH = as in Scottish *loch*. U = as in *book* or *put*. Capital letters signify tone stress.	

Your first and best exercise is to make a translation of this poem. To begin, read aloud the English transliteration, with its marked stresses, a couple of times. Now read the literal (ignoring the notes). Read the literal through again and compare it with the transliteration. Can you see which words are repeated, and must correspond to the repetitions in the literal? Pause to consider the feeling and tone of the literal as a whole. What kind of poem is it? What do its setting and what it has to say suggest to you: does it feel archetypal, or archaic? How would you stage it, if this were in a play?

Now make a translation out of the literal. At first, this doesn't mean anything more than sorting out the English. Some of the grammar is un-English, isn't it? As you work through the lines trying to make your version read as if it wasn't produced by a translation machine, keep an eye on the notes. Other problems come up: ambiguities that need to be resolved, or resonances you ought to try and preserve. Gradually you get a sense that translation is simply a matter of clearing away problems, to get to the real poem lying behind them. It is, in short, exactly like redrafting. Except that in translation you have the original – usually by someone famous or at least a poet you admire – there like a kind of mentor: constantly challenging you to do better, and showing you just how high to aim.

To practise more widely, find a shortish poem, one in which you can spot where everything in the original is. Middle English, or Scots, poems often have a brief glossary at the bottom of the page, because the language is almost close enough for us to understand. Usefully, too, publishers who can afford it print poems in parallel text, with the original on the page facing the translation. For most Western European languages – even without a dictionary, but using the translation provided as a crib – it's reasonably easy to see where each noun, verb and conjunction occurs in the original, not least because English, being a melting-pot tongue, serves as a rough guide to some of the vocabulary. This allows you to see the *structure* of the thought in the original, rather than simply relying on the way it's been teased out in any existing translation. It's this original voice you're translating. Try to read the poem aloud in the original. It should give you a sense of metre and form, but also of the *voice*. Are there long, sonorous, alliterative lines – or fleeting, breathy phrases? Is the voice measured and regular, or is the original in a very flexible free-verse? What can you tell about register and inflexions of meaning from any etymological roots shared between the original vocabulary and English? Is the poem largely abstract, or full of concrete images? Are its verb forms predominantly active or passive, and what does this suggest about the mood of the piece? Now you have a sense of the character of the original, you will be able to juxtapose this with the crib, the glossary, and the literal word-by-word translation that you should go ahead and make. This is the second stage of your work with the piece.

This stage can feel frustrating: try to think of it as deferred gratification. My own interest in translation was awakened by working in just this painstaking way from a language I didn't know then and don't now. Anglo-Saxon was taught at my university as a literature, not a language. Yet at the same time we had to translate the canon ourselves, using only the glossary provided. Although I started out hating this process – I thought, 'Why can't we just read a translation?' – by the end of the year I understood that without this so-called 'finger-work' we'd have found out nothing about the poetry itself, and how it works. Translating is the most intimate way to get to know the work of a poet you admire – because you have to make it your own.

Leaving aside questions about whether you should echo the metre of the original, and how 'foreign' the end product should or should not sound – though contentious in translation studies, these are actually matters of personal literary taste – whenever you try to translate to your own satisfaction, you will end up having to solve the same problems as the original. How can you, too, find a way to say that thing about doves – and using onomatopoeic vowels? How can you explain as concisely as the original does, when English has all the lumber of constructions in place of mere suffixes? As you find yourself re-solving his original problems, you realize you're enacting just what the original poet did. Like an art student sent to a gallery to draw the Old Masters, you can learn how to write by passing poems you admire through the workshop of your own drafting process. As you do so, you can feel connected to the wider world of poetry; a community of traditions in which you're taking your place. Incidentally, if you do find yourself drawn to translating poetry as more than an exercise, there will always be opportunities to publish. Poetry in translation, though under-valued in Britain, is in short supply.

Practitioners with a genuine interest in and feel for it are always needed.

16 The Ideal Reader

Reader, I married him.

Charlotte Bronte, *Jane Eyre*

For whom do you write? Whom do you imagine reading your poems – or would you most like to see reading them? Who sticks in your mind like an internal censor, the figure before whom you'd most hate to make a fool of yourself? Who stops you being honest in your work? Whose comment about your writing has most struck you recently, whether positively or negatively?

The Russian Marxist V.N. Voloshinov said that 'the word is a two-sided act . . . I give myself verbal shape from another's point of view'. This is a useful description of how, when we write, we *are* self-conscious – but in an unusual way. There's something reflexive in that self-consciousness. It seems to go *somewhere else* before it returns to us. Of course most of the time we're just trying to write a poem, not theorize the process. Nevertheless, this problem has always interested writers, not least because it seems to have to do with the nature of writing itself. And writers always want to know more about that, so they can develop what they're doing.

Put simply, writing *is* different from just thinking, even though you think up what you write down. Thinking is intrinsically private – no one can *really* 'read your thoughts' – whereas writing is intrinsically public. Once something's written down, there's always the risk that someone will read it – as we see in everything from data protection scandals to spy stories. That risk may be small (if you live alone, and burn all your drafts, for example), but remains intrinsic to the difference between thinking of a great line and writing it down. Coleridge's dream only became the *poem* 'Kubla Khan' when he wrote it down (which is why that famous interruption by the 'person on business from Porlock' matters so much).

The page is, among other things, a kind of stage on which we can 'show off', inventing – or becoming – the kind of person we would like to be. But this ideal self, or persona, which we write into being – as if it were a fictional character – is oddly similar to the *true* self that we are, according to Oscar Wilde, only when we're loved. He says we become our best self in the eye of that beholder. This means that everything we write is a kind of love letter to, or at least a courtship of, an Ideal Reader. Patricia Duncker's first novel, *Hallucinating Foucault*, is about this love affair between a writer and his Ideal Reader. We start by seeing the reader fall in love with the writer, but soon find it happening in the other direction too. As Duncker's protagonist, a French philosopher she calls Henri Michel, says: 'It is absolutely essential to fall in love with your Muse. For most writers the beloved reader and the Muse are the same person. They should be.' Duncker's novel is an inspiring read for anyone who writes. It also suggests some of the dangers of the relationship between writer and reader, which it implies can be a sort of *folie à deux*.

All the same, what we write needs to include, and to seduce, the reader. We can use the thought of that reader to keep our writing in the shared social world. The enemy of good writing is daydreaming – and the bottom drawer. If you're only writing *for yourself*, however much you believe you'd like to write well, you're locked in a private activity that is as different from writing as what a disturbed individual mutters under his breath is from conversation.

Nevertheless, Jean-Paul Sartre claimed that we are all our own Ideal Readers: because only the author of a text possesses the exact hinterland of resonances and knowledge in which

167

that text sits. The claim often made is that poetry is lost in translation because one language can never exactly mirror the cultural concepts of another. Related to this is the practice of writing *for* a particular audience, whether in genre fiction or – something poets usually have more chance to become familiar with – in reviewing, a discipline which uses terms that differ between broadsheet and specialist press. Conceivably, this could be extended to mean that Wendy Cope's audience and J.H. Prynne's don't overlap – and that each writes only for their own. However, does a poem really only address an audience whose educational and cultural background and interests tally with the author's? And if so, how are so many contemporary readers familiar with, and moved by, the work of Dante or Chaucer?

There are so many things wrong with Sartre's position that we could say it's inside out. It's usually salutary to be edited, or at least read, by someone else who can point out that a passage makes no sense, a resonance is inaudible or overwhelmingly loud (an inadvertent double entendre, for example), or a whole piece of information is missing. The poem, after all, has to work without the 'footnotes' supplied by other material within the poet's own mind, such as memories or private associations.

On the other hand, the Ideal Reader *is* certainly part of our internal, rather than our external, reality. This figure is a strange hybrid: both the individual, whether actual or imagined, whom we feel is our *best* reader – the one who sees the most clearly what our poems are doing – and the *Platonic* Ideal of a reader, or what we think readers in general are. So the person we imagine reading our work is on the one hand an omniscient figure – a sort of kind parent ideally able to understand us, perhaps even better than we understand ourselves – and, on the other, something of a world-out-there Everyman: indifferent, perhaps uncomprehending, and certainly not predisposed to generous understanding.

This paradox produces a tension in the way we experience ourselves as writers. We feel both visible and ignored, over-

and under-appreciated. All poets seem to experience this, whatever their level of success. Every poem is a form of address: because that's what language is. As the philosopher Ludwig Wittgenstein pointed out, there's no such thing as a private language. If I were to have a language entirely my own (and not dependent on existing language, as translation of my mother tongue into a parallel, private vocabulary would be), how would I know that I wasn't changing its term every time I used it? Language needs a hook into the world beyond the self, and that can only be supplied by *another* self. So language is an inherently collective practice. Every time we use language we do so in a collective context: this is even true of the private diary you keep locked away. When you write it, you're *addressing* your own future, past or present self: and you do so in the awareness that other people *could understand* it, if they ever had access to it. The Ideal Reader is the outcome of always knowing that there are other people who understand the language you use.

This being so, it matters how you picture that ideal. Internalize the *really nice* members of your writing group, or people who come along every fourth Tuesday to a read-around in the pub, and you'll internalize an ideal who is too easily pleased. You'll start writing slackly. Internalize the most rigorous poet in the country, whom you once heard read and who has a reputation for being a hard and demanding taskmaster, on the other hand, and you might raise your game marvellously. But having too scary an ideal is a risky strategy. If your current internal reader is someone who was very demanding in your past – what Freud would call a superego, the person whose internalized criticisms still make you unconfident in a whole range of settings – you need to replace that figure with a more generous model.

Choosing a new Ideal Reader is a relatively simple process. First, work out what message your current Ideal Reader is giving you. Just settle down to write, perhaps free-writing, and you'll immediately find whom you imagine you're writing to. Notice how that makes you feel. Ask yourself where, on a scale of one to ten, you'd put that feeling, if number *one* means feeling you're so useless you should give up writing and *ten* is being certain that you're a major poet. Neither of these extremes is of any use, of course. You should probably be aiming for an internalized ideal that feels like a *five* to *six*: as though you're doing OK, but if you stretched yourself you might be able to come up with something they'd really respect. You need to imagine someone believing enough in your potential, and bothering enough with every detail, to really notice your work. You want an image of someone who won't let anything slip past them, but who's delighted by the things you do well. An Ideal Reader should keep you on your toes without knocking you off your stride. If he or she doesn't, then it's time to flick through your mental little black book and think who has inspired and believed in you – and also stretched you. If no one has – if, like many of us, you've developed in isolation – then who do you feel *would*? It's quite normal and acceptable for poets to internalize an established figure – whether poet or editor – as their 'guiding light'. In fact, it's no stranger than any other form of relationship we have with those whose work we read without ever having met them. We imagine them: and in so doing, to some degree we appropriate them.

Since the Ideal Reader you pick will also serve as a kind of model, I'd suggest it could be important to think about gender, ethnicity, sexuality and even age. That sounds strange! But a model *models practice*. This means that you need a sense of your Ideal Reader as a precursor who has solved *equivalent* problems (such as writing against or within a tradition, or devizing a new voice for contemporary material) to the ones you find yourself trying to solve in your own work. It's possible, for example, that if you're a second-generation British-Asian you might have more in common *as a writer* with poets who emerged from *other* hybrid positions – even, for example, that of a native Welsh-speaker writing in English – than with a recent immigrant from the very city your parents were born in. If you're a young woman with children, you could have more in common with a more mature writer, especially another woman, than with your contemporaries. (Or you may not – that's for you to know.)

In other words, it's important to pay attention to your *own* needs, and not simply to assume that the most famous poets writing today will make the best models. The Ideal Reader is the 'person' to whom everything you write is addressed; indeed is, as Duncker says, a kind of love letter. In the end, he or she is a function of your own ego, albeit a necessary one. All writing is carried out in dialogue with the sum of writing: with the tradition and with one's peers. In 'Tradition and the Individual Talent', T.S. Eliot said that the poet becomes a poet by recognizing their precursor somewhere in the existing canon. The emerging poet reads what someone else has already written and thinks, not exactly, 'I can do that' but 'That's me!' They become, in effect, that previous poet's Ideal Reader – and their image of that poet becomes theirs.

Arguably, it's easiest to feel this going on when you write in strict form. A sonnet written today *answers* the sonnets of earlier great poets. It's impossible not to compare them, seeing the form evolve and adapt as vocabulary and register change over the decades. When you write one, you place it alongside those you admire as you look for models and solutions. The form does this for you. But, by extension, *every* poem you write places itself alongside the canon, whatever your conscious thoughts about tradition.

At times, this dialogue becomes something you *actively* engage in. Some poems take off from where the 'work' of an earlier poet left off. For example, Simon Armitage and Glyn Maxwell went to Iceland in 1996 to write *Moon Country*, their echo of W.H. Auden and Christopher Isherwood's 1937 *Letters from Iceland*. Elsewhere, Herbert Lomas's poem is one of many that respond to 'Adlestrop', using the same form and elegiac atmosphere to record his own summer visit to the Cotswold village Edward Thomas made famous. Its first stanza juxtaposes quotations from the original with contemporary detail that parallels it: a car has replaced the steam train –

I too remember Aldestrop –
that compatible weekend in the car
when all the birds of Gloucestershire
seemed intoxicated by tar

('Remembering Adlestrop')

It's this level of detail that makes a response convincing. Tom Paulin's 'versions' of European poems, on the other hand, work – though they are controversial – because they systematically bring in anachronistic or geographically subversive Irish details to what is primarily a form of translation. A version of the Italian poet Eugenio Montale includes the Black and Tans; Mallarmé has the deliberate anachronism 'snot-rag'. Again, it's detail, however subversive, that makes the new poems work. It's not just that one must always enter thoroughly into writing. Here, transformation means the poem has been thoroughly worked over. There's nothing passive for example, in the rendering which steals one of Rilke's most famous lyrics, 'The Swan', for Ireland:

A drudge on piecework cackfooted he bumbles clumsily
on the solid ground a plodder – wally – 's a lunkhead
who wouldn't know a telos if he touched it

Some poems are a kind of imitation of or homage to one already written – they may not translate it, but they answer it, as U.A. Fanthorpe's 'Seminar: Felicity and Mr Frost' does. Carol Ann Duffy's *The World's Wife* has the wives of famous figures like Midas tell their side of the story. The results subvert, but don't lose sight of, the original myth or biography. But this kind of retrieval can also be very serious. The poet Adrienne Rich was consciously *Diving into the Wreck*, in her 1973 collection of poems about how to construct an identity *within* a culture that both restricts and informs the individual. Her famous title poem, which starts 'First having read the book of myths / and loaded the camera, / and checked the edge of the knife-blade, I put on / the body-armor of black

172

rubber / the absurd flippers / the grave and awkward mask', is about this *process*, which all writers have to undergo. Hers is an *ars poetica* that every poet, whatever their cultural position, should read.

Finally, poems enter into dialogue with a canon of texts when they quote from it, as T.S. Eliot famously does in the *Four Quartets*. All these forms of dialogue, whether or not overt, configure our own poetic voice and identity. They are one of the most immediate ways in which we can locate work. A poem should identify itself: it shouldn't need a manifesto or an excuse to accompany it on to the printed page. (This is not to say that manifestos are a bad thing. But they accompany a whole movement, articulating what several poets and poems have *in common*, not explaining an individual poem.) Most poems are about *anything* other than poem-making. A poem will always carry traces of the poet's individual poetic consciousness, but it won't usually present itself in relationship to the canon. However, its poetics will be the result of what the poet has already digested about the nature of poetry – including that canon.

A good way to get a feel for this is to write a poem that explicitly responds to either a particular poem or a single poet's work: one you know well. That response could be parody, re-telling, narrative or discursive prequel or sequel, or explicit address. Pick just one of these: a poem that tries to do several at once will probably fail. Also remember that by far the most interesting parodies, and the most useful for the poet writing them, are affectionate ones. Cruelty is rarely accurate and attentive. It tends to be more concerned with appropriating material than a close-worked line-by-line interrogation of an original. However, even parody doesn't need to adopt a form identical to that of the original. Sometimes, using one form to parody another can produce the funniest and most subtle results. In Wendy Cope's *Making Cocoa for Kingsley Amis*, tightly controlled short poems wittily *encapsulate* their originals. Tight forms allow the poet to be outrageously playful, but at the same time disciplined.

Another kind of dialogue is homage to a genre. A poem like W.H. Auden's 'Where Are You Going?' pays its respects to the whole genre of folk song; like Auden's 'As I Walked Out One Evening', A.E. Housman's book *A Shropshire Lad* is a homage to the ballad. These poems aren't kitsch; they genuinely inhabit their own emotions and narrative. They also re-inhabit and reinvigorate material that isn't currently much used for poem-making: not least because these are collective, oral forms, not traditionally the work of individual poets. James Fenton often writes poems that are half sea-shanty, half-W.S. Gilbert. His *Oxford Book of Love Poems* showed us his locker of tastes and influences. The poems he writes in strict, chant-able form are a kind of homage to a particular register of English verse that tells human truths with wry, extroverted mannerisms: in the tradition of the novelist-poets G.K. Chesterton and Rudyard Kipling and, earlier, of such public satirists as Swift and Pope. The truths they pick on tend to be collective and *public*. They aim to be universally accessible, as the regular metre, with its choruses, suggests. This is poetry that wants to be remembered and quoted both in pubs and on public occasions.

A third, equally powerful, form of poetic dialogue is the one with your peers. Some of this is internal and imaginative dialogue with the *writing*, much as with that of earlier poets. But some is with the actual individuals. Most (though not all) poets develop at least one or two relationships, and maybe a whole circle of poet-friends, where they share their work. Poets have always read each other's writing: with excitement and curiosity, trust and intimacy. A poet who is good enough to be your equal – but not *too* good, so that you offer them little in return and the relationship can't be wholehearted – is like a running mate. You can spur each other on, even by competition. All you need is to be serious enough about your own writing to understand the *detailed* quality of the feedback you need to give and receive. We can 'see' work that we don't know much more clearly than we see our own. Writing which is dull, over-explanatory or confused is much more readily apparent to someone who hasn't written it. Identifying which lines really work is also easier in someone else's work than your own. With practice, it gets easier to articulate *exactly* what you like and so why that works. This close reading is excellent practice for editing your own work – and perhaps, in some professional capacity, other people's. I learnt to be an editor through identifying what worked and what didn't in the poetry of close friends.

These writing peers may become a group, a movement – or simply pals. They may also turn into Ideal Readers. If so, they will intersect with what you write on many different levels. Once you've chosen your new Ideal Reader(s), keep reminding yourself to think about them as you write. Try reading a poem you've written, but are uncertain about, aloud. Imagine you read it to first one, then another, of your Ideal Readers: a peer, a family member or neighbour who likes to read, a well-known contemporary poet. As you read it aloud each time, imagine that Ideal Reader listening. What would you hate them to hear? What would you be proud for them to read? Does this shift from reader to reader? Appropriating their skills and judgement like this is what makes the Ideal Reader such a powerful accompaniment to your writing process.

17 On difficulty

Once, halfway through the journey of our life,
I found myself inside a shadowy wood,
Because the proper road had disappeared.

Sean O'Brien, *Dante's Inferno*

The best poets are always the bravest, though not necessarily
the most experimental. It's never good for a poem (however
helpful it probably is to the poet) to omit something out of
fear. And there are many kinds: the fear that what's divulged
may harm the poem's author, or people in his life; fear of what
the *process* of writing the poem might mean facing up to; fear,
too, of being controversial in form or content; even fear of the
sheer effort involved in honest, exploratory writing.

On the other hand, perhaps this is reasonable. Aren't some
things more important than a poem? Was Osip Mandelstam,
already under suspicion, wise to compose – let alone read out
– the poem parodying Stalin that got him sent to his death in
a Labour Camp? What about persecuted writers who continue
to publish knowing that, if they're condemned, their families
will suffer too? Luckily most of us don't have to face such
challenges. But we *do* write in the contexts of our own lives,
which may cast a poem into doubt. The late Caribbean poet
E.A. Markham wrote that 'our friends die so that we can make
poems'. He meant that writers have a terrible tendency to
make the people they know instrumental to their work.
Writers may subsume the real human experience of those they

know, even those they are closest to.

U.A. Fanthorpe's 'The Poet's Companion' is a characteristically funny and wise poem about the cost of being a poet's wife:

> In public will lead
> The laughter, applause, the unbearably moving silence.
> Must sustain with grace
>
> The role of Muse, with even more grace the existence
> Of another eight or so, also camera's curious peeping
> When the poet is reading a particularly
>
> Randy poem about her, or (worse) about someone else.

Of course, not to acknowledge love in a poem about a beloved is false consciousness: bad for the relationship, bad for oneself – and bad for the poem, too. But it does seem to me that there are certain poems that can't be written – at least not while their subject is alive. Apart from anything else, if you have a shred of compassion you have the potential hurt you're causing at the back of your mind as you work; and the result will be constricted by this in one way or another. Your poem won't be a full expression of what it sets out to explore.

I used to work with writing in hospitals, psychiatric units, prisons and other care settings. I had many shocking, moving and deeply formative experiences: especially individual, human encounters. But to write about the people I met seemed like voyeurism. It could have violated professional codes of confidentiality. More than that, it would have meant *using* the people I was there *for*. On the other hand, there were profound gaps in my work as a result. Other poets presumably have to think carefully before writing about directly personal material, such as an affair, or a family secret. The title poems of Sarah Maguire's first two collections, *Spilt Milk* and *Invisible Mender*, for example, deal with each of these. Jackie Kay has written extensively about the experience of cross-race adoption, most famously in *The Adoption Papers*, while Pascale Petit writes about being abused in *The Zoo Father*.

One solution to the problem of the impermissible poem might be to write for the bottom drawer, which can indeed function like a dowry. When the time is right, there may turn out to be all sorts of good things stored there ready for publication. On the other hand, the whole thrust of *this* book is towards *making it real*. The poem needs to be able to 'go out there': which means being *read*. Arguably, a poem is only completed when it's read by someone else. So this is a matter of individual discretion. Will you benefit more from exploring highly emotional material and the techniques you can use to write from it – techniques and feelings you may later be able to bring to other material? Or do you have so little time that it's important to concentrate on poems that can be read by other people straightaway, allowing you to acquire both a sense of poetic reality and, ideally, feedback?

Pieces that might hurt their subject offer a clear example of what happens when you write from difficult material. At some level you're having an emotion you 'ought not to have', and these poems can only be written if you work with, and overcome, certain internal resistances. Arguably, all such resistances come back to *something you don't want to admit to yourself*: whether that's something you don't like about yourself, or that you don't think you can cope with. The best poems do come from Eliot's 'raids on the inarticulate', which manage to get a little way into what can't be said. The opposite of an emotional 'spill', rant or undigested journal-keeping, these 'raids' push on past what we already *know* we're experiencing, into the roots of emotions, their causes or paradoxical undersides: where we may discover ambivalence, or insight. For example, Sylvia Plath's last great poems, though they *articulate* despair, aren't a *diary* of her emotions over the last few weeks of her life. Apart from anything else, someone who is in despair does not make poems. Instead, these poems derive their power from the way they drag up symbols from the *un*conscious, from what was *not* known.

Such dragging up requires real concentration and profound imaginative resource. In their force and jaggedness, we can see something of the way in which these poems, though written quickly, feel hard-won; as if resistance did indeed form part of the process.

Great philosophical – often metaphysical – poets, from Thomas Traherne and Henry Vaughan to the contemporary Americans Brigit Pegeen Keelly or Mary Oliver, also go some distance into what hadn't been said before because it was difficult *to* say. Partly this is a technical difficulty. Language is a conceptual system, and it's hard to put into words an idea that hasn't been conceptualized before. Poets like Theodor Roethke and Wallace Stevens can seem strange because they say things that no one else has thought. But it's also scary to contemplate what lies beyond appearances, and it's no surprise that poets often want to resist such contemplation. In that resistance, though, lies the secret of success. Like the charisma that surrounds very shy people, difficulty gives poems an extra glow, an intensity and freshness.

Such difficulty may or may *not* be reflected in how difficult the finished poem is to read. Psychoanalysis has an essentially developmental view of the psyche, and Melanie Klein joins Julia Kristeva in arguing that, since we all start out pre-verbal, our most fundamental selves remain, in a sense, pre-verbal. This babble of infancy, which may be expressive (happy hums) but does not *name* the world, bubbles up when we are disturbed and distressed. A more familiar way to say this might be that *I can't put into words* what is very shocking or difficult for me to accept.

There's something in the idea that straightforwardly linear, realist narrative, or regular diction, fail at moments of crisis and intensity. Poems that deal with difficult material *may* be linguistically complex or unorthodox, *either* because the material they deal with isn't fully worked through or because they are attempting to reproduce either the crisis of realization or the essential unsayability of what they deal with. The great Romanian poet Paul Celan, whose mother-tongue like that of other Transylvanians was German, wrote many of his poems of Holocaust survival in fractured German, full of breakage in grammar and image-structure, neologism and unexpected metre. Even the famous 'Death Fugue' relies on repetition for its lamenting effect. These poems tell us not only that the Holocaust is essentially untellable, but that the German language was unbearable to the poet condemned to use it. (Celan killed himself in 1970.)

Theodor Adorno, the German philosopher who famously said that there can be no poetry after the Holocaust, was wrong. Poetry does not necessarily sort out, make sense of and beautify. It can also articulate difficulty itself. One of the most striking of today's poets of difficulty, Jorie Graham, gives us poems in which a poetic narrator *tries* to make sense of war (including the D-Day landings in *Overlord*, and a striking Holocaust poem called 'History'), love, and a God-shaped absence. These are poems that portray human consciousness as something in process, rather than as a series of conclusions:

> I don't know where to start. I don't think my face
> in my hands is right. Please don't let us destroy
> Your world. No *the* world. I know I know nothing. I know I
> can't use you like this. It feels better if I'm on
> my knees, if my eyes are pressed shut so I can see
> the other things, the tiniest ones. Which can still escape
> us. Am I human. Please show me mercy. No please show
> a way.
>
> (from 'Praying (Attempt of May 9 '03)')

Of course, to write in this register about smaller problems (such as desertion by a lover) would be to risk sounding pretentious, but writing from difficulty is important. For one thing, even if the attempt 'fails', it's a necessary counter-balance to poems that attempt to *escape* from what is difficult in life. If you write poems that are nearly all about the beauties of nature, for example, you might ask yourself what's missing: the disappointing marriage, the terrible relationship you have with your daughter, a sense of failure caused by a recent job interview? Everyone writes some happy poems, and it isn't necessary that all your writing should become sad or dull, but it is important that you're explicitly aware of any transcendence or escape-trick you're relying on. Bringing an awareness of the darker side of your experience to bear alongside that transcendence should give you a kick-start, and act as an intensifier, even for your more celebratory work.

However, during my years of working with poetry in health and social care, I saw how dangerously upsetting writing – even thinking – about difficult material can be. People who are in a truly vulnerable position or mood should not be forced to think about what they find hard to face. My workshops always took a theme, and poetic examples, that were spacious enough to allow people to be as honest, or not, as they wished. Working alone presents some risks here. On the other hand, the dark materials are often where the true poetic self lies. For example, I've learnt that my own true writing self isn't the one engaged by themes of light and beauty, music and history. It's a profoundly pessimistic persona, which returns to themes of loss and death. But this shadow side also intensifies my more optimistic, expansive pieces and, I hope, stops them becoming too sweet. So one way to think about your own difficult material is to approach it gently, stopping wherever you feel upset. On the other hand, you can easily find you've bitten off more than you can chew. As we saw in Chapter 12, it's important to know whom to ring if you get upset. It might be, for example, that your partner isn't the person best placed to help you with these emotions, even if they're in the next room. If you know you have a major issue in your life – such as a bereavement, or childhood abuse – you might also make sure you know which specialist organizations (starting with the Samaritans) can offer you support. Even if you don't intend to write about the really difficult things in your life, it's surprising (and also not surprising) how often exploring one thing can stir up another. Promise yourself that you won't be afraid to use such support systems.

If you accept their availability now, you're less likely to tell yourself you don't need them later, when in fact you may. Remember, too, that *you* are the expert on *yourself*. It's for you to decide what you can and cannot face writing. Don't be afraid to start – but don't be afraid to stop, either.

A first step, then, is to list whatever you think are likely to be difficult – emotive – topics for you. These can range from childhood experiences to existential panic. As you list them, notice which ones feel *active*: which still give you a pang. Now put this *conscious* list aside and, setting a timer for eight or ten minutes, brainstorm as many difficult areas and topics as you can think of, scribbling them all down. You may need to ask yourself direct questions, such as: 'What am I afraid of?' or 'Why aren't I happy?' As with all free writing exercises (even though this is a list, not a piece of text), keep the pen moving. When you read this second list back, you'll probably find topics scrambled up, aspects and details mixed together, emotions explicitly named alongside private references such as the name of your partner's best friend, and wide variation in intensity. You'll probably also find repetition. Try to read this list as if you were a stranger. What does it show you about the person it portrays? What personae appear? What is unexpected? How does it compare to the conscious list – not just in terms of topics, but in terms of the person who emerges from it?

This is your difficult material. It's like a larder from which you can help yourself – but only sparingly, as if you were hungry. You might use imagery or resonances from these personal areas to add flavour to your writing in general. You could free-associate round just one thing on your list. You may write a poem that addresses one of the people you associate with this difficult material, *not* explicitly discussing whatever has gone wrong between you (their violence or their illness) but simply as the *addressee* of a poem you've been wanting to write, and that is probably *about* something completely different. You might just keep the list on your computer and glance at it before writing, or when you're stuck in a poem, to remind yourself of the range and depths of your personal experience and psyche.

One of things that range and experience tell you is to trust your own instincts. You've found ways to assimilate difficulty in your life; you can do the same in poetry. Those instincts will also tell you when to protect yourself and stop. Obey them! During those years with health and social care, I repeatedly came across the debate about whether writing, or reading, poetry can be therapeutic. While reading it can undoubtedly help to articulate strong sadness – and make us feel less alone in it – I'm with the former Director of the Poetry Society of Great Britain, Christina Patterson, who said, 'If you knew as many poets as me, you'd certainly hesitate to say that poetry improves communication skills: or indeed mental health!' Poetry written by people who aren't usually able to make their voices heard is a useful social adjustment: bringing all sorts of benefits, such as respect and attention, for those individuals. But writing poetry is *essentially exploratory*. It's not about healing, but about opening up the wound. Writing poetry won't *necessarily* make you feel better about your difficult experiences. On the other hand, drawing on difficult experiences will probably be good for your poetry.

It all depends on how you do that drawing. Poetry that works from difficulty is no different from any other verse, in that it needs to make what is general or abstract concrete. It's no good writing, 'I feel *so* desperate'. We need, as in any other poem, to know *how* desperate that is; what it feels *like* (try simile or metaphor); and the occasion – *why* and *when*. Sappho's 'Fragment Thirty-One' has survived since antiquity, and in dozens of versions through the centuries since the Renaissance, because it is so good at describing sexual jealousy. (In Anne Carson's version, in *If Not, Winter*, this key passage reads 'and cold sweat holds me and shaking / grips me all, greener than grass / I am and dead'.)

Among contemporary poets, Elaine Feinstein, in *Talking to the Dead*, addresses not only her late husband, but widowhood itself. She uses simple, strong and dignified diction to spell out what she feels:

... my story as a wife
is threaded on the string of my own life,

and when I touch these beads, I still remember
your warm back as we slept like spoons together.

('Widow's Necklace')

Penny Shuttle's *Redgrove's Wife*, named for her late husband the poet Peter Redgrove, explores similar ground using almost the same quasi-shamanistic poetics for which he was famous, as if to summon him up. Their poetic territory always overlapped strikingly, and these poems seem to speak for both partners in the tragedy:

A poem stays awake long after midnight
talking you from room to room,
does not care that walls have ears,
les parades oyen

A poem prefers tin to silver
. . .

('Poem')

Emotion is welcome – we've got beyond the fashion for Cool, in other words – even though it needs to *earn its place*. Naming an emotion, without showing it to us, is just like naming any other abstraction. With practice, though, you can become a connoisseur of emotions, able to distinguish tiny variations between them. Is that malice you're feeling, or just spite? How intensely felt is your loyalty? What's the difference between desire and lust? The best way to develop this connoisseurship is to keep a poetry diary. It may not include any verse itself, but will be a place where you practise defining with ever-greater precision, and ever-more-uncannily precise imagery, the precise shades of each waxing and waning emotion. Armed with this emotional glossary, you can explore difficult topics at your leisure and with detachment, away from the heat of *experience*. And, just like your list of topics, this glossary will be a resource for *all* your poetry.

18 Jackanory:
narrative verse

I'll tell you a story
About Jack-a-nory

Anon

Narrative has been part of poetry from the earliest times. The
first named poets include Homer and Virgil. The great
Mesopotamian epic *Gilgamesh*, written more than 1,000 years
BCE and thus 1,000 years older than the *Iliad*, is told in verse.
Much ethnographic poetic material from Europe is also narra-
tive. The Finnish *Kalevala* was reconstructed in the nineteenth
century by Elias Lonnrot; Norse and Old High German sagas
informed Wagner's *Ring Cycle*; the Anglo-Saxon *Beowulf* is a
long poem about heroism.

Our folk material also includes the Border Ballads: master-
pieces of compression, as are our often-narrative folk songs,
with their stories of abandonment and loss. Think of 'The
Foggy Foggy Dew':

I am a bachelor, I live by myself
And I work at the weaver's trade
And the only, only thing that I ever did wrong
Was to woo a fair young maid.
I wooed her in the summer time
And in the winter too

And the only, only thing that I ever did wrong
Was to keep her from the foggy, foggy, dew.

One night she came to my bedside
As I lay fast asleep
She laid her head upon my bed
And she began to weep.
She wept, she cried, she damn near died
She said 'What shall I do?'
So I hauled her into bed and I covered up her head
Just to keep her from the foggy, foggy dew.

Now I am a bachelor, I live with my son
And we work at the weaver's trade.
And every, every time that I look into his eyes
He reminds me of that fair young maid
He reminds me of the summer time
And of the winter too
And of many, many times that I held her in my arms,
Just to keep her from the foggy, foggy dew.

A novelist could take a few hundred pages over this story of illicit love and loss.

Many European countries had founding poets who developed a national literary language from oral dialect at the time of the rise of the nation state, generally in the nineteenth century: they include Mihai Eminescu in Romania, Adam Mickiewicz in Poland and France Prešeren in Slovenia. The poets who are seen as having developed English as a literary language – Chaucer in the fourteenth century and Shakespeare in the sixteenth and seventeenth – did so largely through narrative forms. Chaucer's *Tristan and Isolte* and *Canterbury Tales* arise from a medieval culture of *romans* – long narrative poems of courtly love, chivalry and customary manners. But, unlike the Latin languages such as Occitan in which *romans* were first written, Middle English was also deeply inflected by the (Germanic) Anglo-Saxon out of which it arose, and Chaucer had to develop ways to do what those romances did in a language that had never encountered them before. The extended narrative form, which in turn contained lyric verse, was arguably what developed and expanded Middle English, from which contemporary English is only an adaptation. It might also be argued that the Renaissance English Shakespeare developed and expanded was similarly stretched to its capacity by the demands of verse drama: that Shakespeare, too, had to explore and reassemble the language for narrative purposes.

So here are three models of narrative verse: as epic; in the portable fictions of folk song and ballad; and as an extra set of demands which affect the development of a whole language. As each of these demonstrates, narrative poetry doesn't have to 'skim off' the richness of detail and linguistic pleasure we get from verse. Quite the opposite: it can serve as an intensifier. Every poem tells us something, as well as telling it in a certain way. Often what it has to say is an observation, or a line of thought. In political verse we'd expect this to be a line of argumentation. John Milton, that most political of poets, retains the full sense of *argument* in the criss-crossed, enjambed, lines of his *Paradise Lost*. But a poem can also tell a story of emotion, interaction, action and reaction. These are absorbing, universal themes, and poetry is not diluted, but enriched, by engaging with them.

However, many poets are nervous about writing at length, a concern we'll return to in the next chapter. So it's useful to start by engaging with narrative in miniature. Our model for this is the ballad:

Sir Patrick Spens

The king sits in Dunfermling toune,
Drinking the blude-reid wine:
'O whar will I get guid sailor,
To sail this schip of mine?'

Up and spak an eldern knicht,
Sat at the king's richt kne:
'Sir Patrick Spens is the best sailor
That sails upon the se.'

The king has written a braid letter,
And signd it wi his hand,
And sent it to Sir Patrick Spens,
Was walking on the sand.

The first line that Sir Patrick red,
A loud lauch lauched he;
The next line that Sir Patrick red,
The teir blinded his ee.

'O wha is this has don this deid,
This ill deid don to me,
To send me out this time o' the yeir,
To sail upon the se!'

'Mak haste, mak haste, my mirry men all,
Our guid schip sails the morne:'
'O say na sae, my master deir,
For I feir a deadlie storme.

'Late late yestereen I saw the new moone,
Wi the auld moone in hir arme,
And I feir, I feir, my deir master,
That we will cum to harme.'

O our Scots nobles wer richt laith
To weet their cork-heild schoone;
Bot lang owre a' the play were playd,
Thair hats they swam aboone.

O lang, lang may their ladies sit,
Wi their fans into their hand,

Or eir they se Sir Patrick Spens
Cum sailing to the land.

O lang, lang may the ladies stand,
Wi thair gold kems in their hair,
Waiting for thair ain deir lords,
For they'll se thame na mair.

Haf owre, haf owre to Aberdour,
It's fiftie fadom deip,
And thair lies guid Sir Patrick Spens,
Wi the Scots lords at his feit.

This is a story with enough resonance – of regret and irony, and through identification and recognition on the reader's part – to generate atmosphere however it's told. Try paraphrasing it in a couple of sentences, and you can see how it's these *resonances* which are the bones of the poem.

This paraphrase test is a useful one for any story. If you're thinking of one you'd like to turn into verse, try summing it up in a couple of sentences, as if you were telling it *to* someone. If it doesn't feel important, or resonant, enough when you express it like this, but instead needs lots of qualifiers and explanations to make it work, it probably isn't strong enough for poetry. So what sort of thing *does* work? Here are some examples: A rural childhood is an education in life (Wordsworth's *The Prelude*). Brutalized by witnessing Armenian massacres in the First World War, an Australian serviceman is literally no longer able to feel pain. This gives him such exceptional strength that he sees service in many of the twentieth century's hot-spots, until he's rescued by falling in love (Les Murray, *Fredy Neptune*). Janet's lover has been stolen by the fairies. The only way she can get him back is by waiting for them to ride by at midnight and catching hold of him, no matter what shape he assumes ('Tam Lin'). The affair ends (Hugo Williams's collection, *Billy's Room*).

Two of these stories are from book-length poems, one a folk

190

song, and one a recent collection. Despite variations in form and length, the resonances of each are moral or emotional – and, above all, *interesting*. But the ballad of Sir Patrick Spens has much more to it than story, even though it seems to be nothing *but* story. That paradox is the secret of narrative verse. For whether or not the poem pauses to describe a place or feeling, any description feels part of the trajectory of the whole, infused with the life of poem and story. This has partly to do with register, partly to do with pacing, and partly to do with formal coherence. Think of the opening of Samuel Taylor Coleridge's *The Rime of the Ancient Mariner*:

It is an ancient Mariner,
And he stoppeth one of three.
'By thy long grey beard and glittering eye,
Now wherefore stopp'st thou me?

Because metre and rhyme are already in place, this opening has the same active 'feel' as the actual shipboard action narrated by the ancient mariner. But these opening lines also have something of the character of the main story: a sense of strangeness, of separation from normal life, and of compulsion. Why, after all, *does* the wedding guest stop to listen?

In setting the scene for *Fredy Neptune*, Les Murray gives us his hero's family background as an explanation of time and place but also of character. Yet that scene-setting also bustles with active life, rather than slowing the novel down with merely physical description. This 255-page poem opens:

That was sausage day
on our farm outside Dungog.
There's my father Reinhard Boettcher,
my mother Agnes. There is brother Frank
who died of the brain-burn, meningitis.
There I am having my turn
at the mincer. Cooked meat with parsley and salt
winding out, smooth as gruel, for the weisswurt.

Here's me riding bareback in the sweater
I wore to sea first.

And we're off on his sea-voyages.

In 'Sir Patrick Spens', the scene-setting is even more cursory, and yet perfectly image-building: 'The king sits in Dunfermling toune, / Drinking the blude-reid wine', while Sir Patrick, we're told 'Was walking on the sand'. The ballad also reminds us that a second characteristic of narrative verse is its diction. Since the earlier narrative forms were oral, they existed purely in performance. They're musical and lively to listen to, but they also *sit well* in the mouth. It's a pleasure to say:

The first line that Sir Patrick red,
A loud lauch lauched he;
The next line that Sir Patrick red,
The teir blinded his ee.

As well as the repetition, what's so characteristic and pleasing is the alliteration and assonance: line/ loud/ laugh/ laughed is *broken up*, aptly, by 'the tear'. But now assonance takes over, and it seems it was there all along: next / line / tear / blinded / eye (the Scots spelling shows how close the slant rhyme of teir/ee and blinded/ee is).

Don Paterson writes about being able to pick up a poem, hold it at arm's length, and see by the scattered diversity of letters that it's not a sonic unity:

One of those hellish things you learn after ten years working in editing – I hardly dare confess this – is that you can hold a poem a yard away, and without having read a word know there's a 99% chance that you won't like it. Most often this is because any random two- or three-line passage appears to contain all the letters of the alphabet.

He may be exaggerating his distaste for variety, but clustered assonance and – to a lesser extent, because it's so audible – alliteration both immediately drag a poem into formal unity. Ballads benefit from the unifying effects of rhyme and metre too. Among the lines of alternating iambic quatrameter and tetrameter in 'Sir Patrick opens' , only the second and fourth lines of every stanza rhyme, but because of assonance and alliteration the effect is of real sonic integrity.

Think of twentieth-century ballad poems, such as those by Charles Causley or David Harsent. Causley's 'Ballad of the Bread Man', for example, opens:

> Mary stood in the kitchen
> Baking a loaf of bread.
> An angel flew in through the window.
> 'We've got a job for you,' he said.

> 'God in his big gold heaven,
> Sitting in his big blue chair,
> Wanted a mother for his little son.
> Suddenly saw you there.'

> Mary shook and trembled.
> 'It isn't true what you say.'
> 'Don't say that,' said the angel,
> 'The baby's on the way.'

What you notice first is the clean diction. This has to do with sonic integrity and with something known as *muscularity*; an absence of inflection and hesitation. There aren't many mid-line commas that qualify clauses within these poems. Phrases move straight forward. In fact, getting rid of commas is a useful exercise in itself, even though many poems do need a rich play of punctuation. The ideal poem could, arguably, do it all with words. If you can get grammar, sentence structure and line breaks to do all, or most, of your punctuation, the poem that results should be clear-cut and unhesitating. This particularly suits ballads which, emerging as they do from an aural tradition, need to be memorable and gripping. Clarity allows them to move fast, *miming* the forward-propulsion of their narrative: what E.M. Forster, in *Aspects of the Novel*, calls 'the naked worm of time'.

This chronological 'and then and then' is fundamental to narrative. It needn't be the way a story is organized: flash-back, suspense and stream of consciousness are all *narrative devices* – ways of telling – after all; and they can intensify the story-telling experience. Coleridge's *Mariner*, remember, is telling his story after it's over; Wordsworth's *Prelude* is the story of his childhood narrated by an adult persona. But 'and then and then' *is* the grammar of narrative. Events have a causal relationship to one another; that's what binds them into a story. To take one example, the given circumstance of a character (being stubborn, or susceptible) is what, in the classic formula of tragedy, clashes disastrously with whatever comes to pass. The consequences of an initial bad decision escalate and ramify (as in Thomas Hardy's tragedies *Tess of the d'Urbervilles* or *The Mayor of Casterbridge*: as, too, in such comedies as Kingsley Amis's *Lucky Jim* or Martin Amis's *The Rachel Papers*) and the original deed cannot be redeemed. Character and circumstance are irrevocably incompatible, so that there *is* no existential choice for the protagonist, however much there seems to be (Hardy's *Jude the Obscure* has its roots in classical tragedy from Sophocles to Euripedes). The stages in the tragic narrative – and many traditional ballads are tragedies – are not beads on a string so much as the steps of an escalator. The useful musical sign for this is a *crescendo* (written <). Although in musical performance it is confined to getting louder and not, for example, faster, we can use this term to indicate intensification.

In other words, narrative is trajectory. The story a poem tells has a sense of direction, whatever the order in which it's told. It's important to *own* this fact of narrative in order to keep: a) a sense of priorities. The meaning of a narrative poem *is* the story. In fiction, *what happens* is a single extended metaphor for all the situations that can be read into it; and b) the forward movement of narrative. Characters reveal themselves in *actions*, such as what they say. The narrative poem does not use long descriptive exegesis.

For better or worse, narrative verse has been popular in the past with schoolteachers. It was thought to sugar the pill for children who didn't enjoy poetry itself. This thinking may have been problematic in some respects, but it offers us a useful hint. Narrative gives an *additional* dimension to verse. Among old school favourites are poems by Rudyard Kipling and G.K. Chesterton, 'The boy stood on the burning deck' and 'There's a deathless hush in the quad tonight'. Recent fashion has been to decry writing like this, and in so doing to decry the wider field of narrative verse. Shamelessly rhythmic – no cross-currents of alexandrines or sprung rhythm, none of the latent form of syllabics, here – it's been much parodied. But lazy reading overlooks the fact that, as we saw in Chapter 11, such strict metre is an *intentional* vehicle – for making the work memorizable, among other things. Sometimes it's mimetic. Kipling's military poems, for example, march to the same beat as their protagonists.

Readings that miss the deep relationship between metre and content can fail to recognize other semantic strengths, too. It may be easier to look at folk material in order to see how language that has been winnowed by narrative is heightened and strengthened in order to carry the additional demands of story.

Folk song and ballad embrace repetition. They aren't afraid to use the same name for the same object or character, time and again: they don't worry about synonyms. A castle is a castle all the way through a Border Ballad: it doesn't need to turn into a bastion, a fort or a tower. Tam Lin keeps his name throughout his eponymous ballad – he doesn't become 'Tammy', nor 'our hero'. This chime of repetition is underscored by the use of repeated phrase or chorus, as in this ballad from Northern England:

The Lyke-Wake Dirge

This ae nighte, this ae nighte,
—*Refrain*: Every nighte and alle,
Fire and fleet and candle-lighte,
—*Refrain*: And Christe receive thy saule.

When thou from hence away art past
To Whinny-muir thou com'st at last

If ever thou gavest hosen and shoon,
Sit thee down and put them on;

If hosen and shoon thou ne'er gav'st nane
The whinnes sall prick thee to the bare bane.

From Whinny-muir when thou may'st pass,
To Brig o' Dread thou com'st at last;

From Brig o' Dread when thou may'st pass,
To Purgatory fire thou com'st at last;

If ever thou gavest meat or drink,
The fire sall never make thee shrink;

If meat or drink thou ne'er gav'st nane,
The fire will burn thee to the bare bane;

This ae nighte, this ae nighte,
—*Every nighte and alle,*
Fire and fleet and candle-lighte,
—*And Christe receive thy saule*

This repetition with modulation works in the same way as
it does in a sestina, villanelle or ghazal. It strengthens the
internal musculature of the poem, pulling it together rather
like a poetic pilates. The repeated chorus reminds us how the

interrelatedness of events in a story – a relatedness through entailment, which happens through time – can nevertheless be *thought of* simultaneously. *Every* gesture is qualified by 'Every night and alle' and *every* stage of human life and death is redeemed by 'And Christe receive thy soul'. In the same way, we can't think of Sir Patrick Spens's shipwreck without thinking of that moment at court in which the king, or his elderly adviser, condemns him to the dangerous sea-voyage. Thinking about these two things at the same time is how we experience the overlap of causality.

These capacities of the ballad, and its shorter cousin the folk song, mean both offer poetic resources that are good to master, especially in preparation for writing other forms of narrative verse. To practise writing a ballad deploying all these resources, pick a story that has particular resonance for *you*. The personal is always easier to write well than the political, with its tendency towards generalization. On the other hand, too slight a story – an anecdote from daily life – won't sustain the ballad form, whose clarity takes no hostages, but relentlessly exposes the material it's made of. Since traditional forms *can* be seen as whimsical, aim to tell your story in not too many stanzas: ten or twelve quatrains are probably enough.

As with any borrowing – for in a way you're creating a 'version' of ballad, since your poem is not anonymous and oral but authored – you need to enter into both diction and mode with conviction. The best way to do this is probably through enjoying the *technical* form. After a couple of verses of concentrating on this, you should have a sense of 'ownership' of the emerging poem, much as if you were working in any other literary form. And it's even more important than with any other poem that it passes the 'reading aloud' test: even if you have no actual audience.

Epic verse, meanwhile, often supplied what Plato, in *The Republic*, calls a nation's Foundation Myth. It might relate how the world became, and the central role the nation had in that becoming: or detail the wars by which the first peoples of the nation, and their kings, identified themselves. Epic verse therefore had an explicitly collective, but also an implicitly existential, role. It was *mythopoeic*. Contemporary poets have understood these poetic possibilities for myth. What Philip Larkin disparagingly called, referring to Ted Hughes, the 'myth kitty' is indeed a great resource for imagery and narrative metaphor. It's no surprise that not only Hughes, but also many other poets writing in English, have taken on Ovid's *Metamorphoses*, with their fertile symbols of human identity and difficulty.

As we saw in Chapter 16, when Adrienne Rich 'dived' into the submerged treasure ship of our collective cultural unconscious, in her attempts to create a new Foundation Myth for herself as a woman and a poet (and indeed one with a particular ethnic and sexual identity), she showed us there was no reason why poets shouldn't be magpies, stealing tropes and stories for their own work. Earlier, Federico Garcia Lorca borrowed from flamenco (*cante jondo*) to develop the *duende*, register and indeed iconography of his own vivid verse. Ted Hughes tried to create, in *Crow*, a synthesis of foundation and shamanic myths where a fallen Everyman was more beast than human. And poets like Ioana Ieronim have used 'folk' imagery, in a move not dissimilar to that of Modernist visual artists like Picasso, to explore traumatic events of recent history in the register that material demands.

The connections between your own difficult material and tropes from myth or folk poetry are necessarily *metaphorical* – and therefore irrational. They either work or they don't. The best way to find them is to free-associate loosely around your material from Chapter 17. At first, simply brainstorm. Then ask yourself questions from the Furniture Game: if this feeling/story/territory were a weather/artefact/ colour/religion, what would it be? Such primitive questions are just the start of finding your way into a relationship with myths that will work with your material.

Another approach is to think about ethnographic, religious and mythic material that appeals to you. Ask yourself *why* it seems to speak to you so much. Why does it resonate, and with what? What sense of self does it suggest to you? The myth kitty is, like so much poetic equipment, something to be aware of and keep to hand. But it won't – or shouldn't – be present in *all* your work, and may only appear incidentally, among metaphors from quite other areas of experience. On yet further occasions, it may produce a whole sequence or set of poems.

Epic poetry also makes us think about length. The whole of the next chapter will look at the possibilities of *writing long*. Here it's just worth noting that there's been a revival in English of the verse-novel. In 1986 Vikram Seth published *The Golden Gate*, a novel in chapters made up of multiple sonnets. He transformed the sonnet into an accessible, elegantly narrative form. Meanwhile, Derek Walcott was reworking first the *Odyssey* and then the story of the *Bounty* into rich Caribbean vocabulary and imagery in two great verse novels, *Omeros* and *Bounty*. The Australian Les Murray wrote *Fredy Neptune*, a history of the European century; writing from a palimpsest of personal experience, Craig Raine published *History: The Home Movie* in 1994 – the history in question was partly Russian – and *A la recherche du temps perdu* in 1999. The Canadian Anne Carson has published two verse novels of passionate private life, *Autobiography of Red* and *The Beauty of the Husband*, an anatomy of sexual rejection and jealousy in twenty-four 'tangos'. Glyn Maxwell's *The Sugar Mile* is a book-length narrative set of poems spoken by individuals living through the Blitz. And Ciaran Carson has published a study in blue, shadows and reflections – his palindromic verse-novel *For All We Know* (2008) – which, like Seth's, is written entirely in sonnets.

These books differ profoundly from one another. The verse novel isn't yet a form that is 'set'. It offers the writer extraordinary scope, while also proffering a whole set of questions. Can one write at length without sacrificing lyric intensity? What are the costs and compensations of strict formal or tonal consistency, versus the need for variety, in longer work? Does a book-length poem necessarily tell a story in a *different way* from a prose novel: is it, for example, more reflexive, or tighter in focus? Many of the answers to these questions come from more general thinking about writing at length, and it's to this we now turn.

19 Extended forms: series and sequences

When you set out for Ithaka
Ask that your way be long.
　Constantine Cavafy, trans. E. Keeley and P. Sherrard, 'Ithaka'

When I teach poetry workshops in primary schools, I ask the children to try to define a poem. We usually agree that it has something to do with form ... and topic. ... But the closer they get to a definition, the more it seems to slip away. So I encourage them to think about the way poetry *looks*, instead: how the words don't go right across the page. A poem, I suggest, is *concentrated*. At one level, this is just a way to show children that every word matters. But poetry *always* has to engage with the short sharp shock of the lyric. Lyric poems are, in effect, sprints rather than marathons, even if – to deepen the image for a moment – it's possible that they produce the best runners.

　Concentration and intensity are often exactly what allow one to say what one wants. But not always. Narrative is an obvious example of verse that can't get all its business done in thirty-five or so lines: the standard for British poetry since the advent of poetry competitions. (Most require a poem of fewer than forty lines – but too much shorter and you won't have given yourself room to be heard.) Another exception is what I call *poetry of process*. Poets as varied as D.H. Lawrence, at the turn of the last century in the UK, or Jorie Graham, at the turn of this century in the USA, have given us highly worked and inward-directed studies of *having* an experience, using techniques including stream of consciousness, question, re-statement and the first person pronoun. Such poetry, which questions itself as it goes – and recognizes how radically unstable, how open to suspicion, anything it has to say must be – takes time and poetic space. In general, too, if you mean to write any kind of poetry that isn't prescriptive – for example, about public political issues, or the family you come from – you'll have to be prepared to both understate and undercut your own certainties. Other poets do this by using the 'veil' of *imagery*. And Emily Dickinson's 'tell the whole truth but tell it slant' is highly practical advice. Her own deeply religious poetry often poses its ideas as *questions,* and uses dashes to gasp with uncertainty. It's these 'slanting' techniques that allow her insights to be heard, by believers and non-believers alike. Yet her poems are short. They're also numerous.

Perhaps the really great topics simply can't be encapsulated in a single poem. Shakespeare didn't write just one sonnet and let it do all his thinking about love for a whole lifetime. John Donne and Gerard Manley Hopkins repeatedly address the God they struggle with. We know the cliché that every poem is a failure. That being so, Samuel Beckett's motto, 'Try again, fail again. Fail better', suggests repeated attempts offer us a kind of hope. It can be useful to write *clusters* of poems on a topic. Such clusters may produce one or two poems, not normally the first ones to emerge, which *go further* and *do more* than you knew you could.

A *group* of poems representing different 'goes at' a topic can also be collected as a sequence. Such sequences are distinct poetic entities. Their logic is cumulative, yet each poem has to be able to stand alone. If it's not complete enough it will become, in effect, part of a single long poem. There's nothing artistically invalid about that, either. It's perfectly legitimate to join draft fragments together to form a satisfying whole: whether you simply find an order within which each works as a free-verse stanza; whether you revise and dovetail the sections so that a line from one, for example, ends up attached to another, while a third disappears altogether; or whether you create a new, perhaps more formal, structure in which to embed the material. Whichever way you work, you'll find that assembling a long piece from a jigsaw of fragmentary material really does mean working back *from* the material you've already written. You need to pay close attention to variations in register, and to the possibility of contradictory messages. You also need to make editorial decisions about your own work, noticing which pieces work best – and which are too weak to include. If you don't feel ready to write a cluster of new poems, try looking back through your abandoned drafts. You may well find thematic links between some of them: we all have preoccupations our writing returns to. Take four or five you're pretty sure are never going to go anywhere and see whether you can fit passages that work together into a single longer poem.

Working on a sequence is rather similar to all of this. The main difference is in velocity. Poem sections read much faster than equally short freestanding poems from a sequence. That's both because the breaks (asterisks or numbers) are lighter and more digestible within a poem; and because the incomplete nature of each section pushes the reader on towards completion – into the next section, and the next. Completion – think of the click shut of a sonnet's closing couplet – is a closure of attention, too. There's always a margin of silence or paper at the end of a poem, even within a sequence. So the poems in a sequence have to work autonomously as well as together.

Sequence and section order *may* be roughly chronological – in order of writing – and present a line of developing understanding. You may not, though, have written your poems in the order that you now feel best expresses your ideas. If you're not sure what that 'line of thought' should be, think back to what first interested you about the topic, and follow this thread again. There is, despite the contemporary educational fashion for reading poetry for 'correct' content, *no* correct way for you to approach bereavement, fear of abandonment, or the experience of visiting another society. The only way that will work is *your own*: along the living line of your own relationship to the material. Alternatively, you could chose to layer discursive with more formal material, in order to pace a piece and give it balance and variety. It's important to keep an eye on register, too. There is no point in starting with all your strongly felt material and ending up with a comet's tail of five-finger exercises. Be prepared to interleave, as well as to cut material that simply clutters up your work.

When you have a provisional order, become more ruthless still. Remove any weak sections that simply get in the way. And put 'notes to self' where you can see something is missing. There might be a gap in the argument – such as a missing speaker, or a piece of narrative that would make sense of following sections – or you may see that you need to balance the sequence with a particular poetic texture at a certain point. Next, run through the sequence a few times: not *reading*, just skimming and seeing what follows where and how it works. If you feel relatively happy, write your missing sections. It's a paradox of poetry that the demands of *form* (what the sequence needs) can show you what's missing in your *thought*.

Now look at some models. Wallace Stevens's 'Thirteen ways of looking at a blackbird' – like George MacBeth's homage, 'Thirteen ways of stroking the Peter' – is not a sequence but a single poem built of multiple apperceptions. These read as if they were one single thought – they all move in the same direction – yet their effect, as in a photo-album, is of a single portrait built up from a series of snapshots. Each would not, by itself, encapsulate but only evoke the subject. On the other hand, quasi-narrative *sequences* include the serial everyman poems of John Berryman's *Dream Songs* and Zbignew Herbert's *Mr Cogito*, Alan Brownjohn's *Ludbrooke* and Christopher Reid's *Mr Mouth*. Here, characterization is a matter of gradual accumulation through incident after incident. The sense of many aspects making up the prismatic whole remains. In fact, such sequences benefit from the variety of their approaches. John

Fuller's *The Space of Joy* is bound together by tone and subject matter – a study of European influence in the arts – but, though its eight poems are narrative, they tell different stories. Edgar Lee Masters's *Spoon River Anthology*, which tells the life-stories of a fictional community of individuals, starting from their gravestones, builds up into the portrait of a whole town.

Writing at length has nothing to do with slowing down: quite the reverse. Pace matters even more in longer material, which has to sustain the reader – and itself. Thematic linkage, like repetition, speeds up a poem: unless handled badly, when of course it slows it down. The reader mustn't become bored. We'll see in the next chapter how similar such considerations of order and pace are, in turn, to the process of editing a manuscript. A professional editor, editing an anthology or a magazine, works in just the same way. But this brings us to another question. Since I know that I don't always read a poetry book or magazine in order, to what extent do I *need* to order the sections in a long poem or sequence?

There are two answers to this. First: strictly speaking, some sequences are *series*. The poems run in narrative order, or order of argument, and wouldn't make sense out of this order. Narrative sequences such as *Mr Cogito* and Geoffrey Hill's *Mercian Hymns*, which cover their protagonists' lives from birth to death, are in fact series. But it's also true that even sequences may rely on their *order of exposition*. For example, Ted Hughes's *Crow* starts with various versions and 'Legends' about the birth of Crow, although its trickster battle and love scenes seem to evoke a continuous present of Crow-ness.

The second answer is more existential. Even if the reader *seems* to ignore sequencing, he or she benefits from it subconsciously. There are three reasons for this. First, if the poems that make up a sequence *can't be made to work* in *any* order, they simply don't work as a whole. Possibly, something's missing, or has been disproportionately exaggerated. Second, building a sequence makes a robust entity. Raggedness and imperfection are easily picked up on. If the reader gets bored where the material is a bit thin, or feels unconvinced by the concluding poem, you've lost him. Third, the skimming, browsing eye picks up on a great deal more than we realize. Browsing, or getting the feel of, a book or manuscript prior to a proper reading, entails a flicking between points. In fact, it's a kind of mapping of the sequence as a whole. Proportion, texture, density – the *architecture* of a sequence – can be absorbed even when we read out of order.

This principle is extended yet further when poets publish themed collections. These may not be, strictly speaking, sequences, but rather collections of poems that approach one topic in various ways. In other words, they open and extend the idea of a sequence into something that is slightly less organic, at least in formal terms, yet manages to sustain threads of continuity. Narrative series and formal unity are often less apparent in book-length explorations of a theme. Anne Sexton's *The Awful Rowing Towards God* is a collection of poems, some short and some longer, about her experience of hospitalization for a bipolar disorder after a suicide attempt. Arranged in roughly narrative order, it forms a loose series. This is formally very different from her *Transformations*, which is a set – rather than a series – of fairy tales re-told in roughly matching form and register. Ken Smith's *Wormwood* and Tim Liardet's *The Blood Choir* are both collections of poems about working in prisons. Yves Bonnefoy's *On the Movement and Immobility of Douve* is a study of illness and bereavement which, like Penny Shuttle's *Redgrove's Wife* and Elaine Feinstein's *Talking to the Dead*, also broadens that topic (to universal mutability in Bonnefoy's work, a chaotic contemporary world in Shuttle's, and the long history of European anti-Semitism in Feinstein's). Louise Glück's *The House on Marshland* explores family life. Fred D'Aguiar's *Airy Hall* includes a title sequence set in rural Guyana. Selima Hill writes collections that are not only thematically linked, but sometimes even repeat a trope throughout; as in 2002's *Portrait of my Lover as a Horse*, all of whose titles start, 'Portrait of my Lover as—'

This takes us to the boundary of basic questions about the coherence of a collection, which we'll look at in the next chapter. There *is* an increasing fashion for thematically unified books, even if that unity is primarily generated by the particular preoccupations of the three or so years in which a book was written. Perhaps this unity is simply more advertised than it used to be. In the 1970s and 1980s, Ted Hughes was relatively unusual, in the UK, in publishing what I call book-length collections – poems entirely dedicated to one topic but not sequential – such as *Moortown Diary* and *Elmet.*

This brings us back to the idea of the book-length poem. John Milton's *Paradise Lost*, Wordsworth's *The Prelude*, Blake's visionary books, Louis MacNeice's *Autumn Journal* and W.H. Auden's *New Year Letter* – respectively, biblical exegesis, memoir, vision, journal and confession – are all great examples of a form that need not be quite a verse novel in the straight-forwardly fictional sense.

One of the great under-discussed problems of writing poetry is how to find a topic when you feel like writing. The feeling of wanting to write doesn't necessarily come accompanied by a first line. Instead, there's a sense of resource and latency. Theoretically, it ought to be possible to write about *anything*, quite arbitrarily. After all, the whole world is dense with fascination, texture, science, paradox, cultural meaning and our relationships with this. But the truth is that only some of these things work for each of us on any given day – at least as a trigger into that authentic engagement which will produce a real poem. Conversely, it's possible to care deeply about something but to have a too worked-out position, or too many pressing questions about it, to be able to turn that into a poem. Poetry workshops use exercises to generate new poems. As we've seen, these are often unable to provoke real personal poetic necessity. Although for some people being required to write within a workshop is the only way to 'get down to it', bringing the exercise technique to your own work desk can be problematic.

Working on a long piece – providing it does engage with you and your concerns – solves this problem. Every time you've a chance to write, you can return to a project that you've already chosen and that you know interests you. You don't have to cast around for a starting point. Anyone who has written a book of any kind knows the pleasure and relief of knowing where you are every time you return to your desk.

Writing at length also allows you to go further into a subject: beyond the foreclosure of a conventional ending. Craig Raine's suggestive title *The Onion, Memory* reminds us that concentration should push through the layers of what we think we know to the next ring – and the next. Because of this, trying to write long does *not* spoil you for writing to conventional length. Instead, it raises your game within those forms. Once you've written *past* the 'dying fall' of a conventional conclusion, you're less likely to foreclose on your material, and your own personal resources, again.

The best way to try out writing to length is to have in mind your own 'difficult material', or topics of absorbing interest (from post-industrial society to meditation), as you read through possible models. Look out long poems by, for example, Allen Ginsberg, Gary Snyder, Kenneth Koch and Basil Bunting. Marina Tsvetaeva's long poems are wonderful in translation, as are those of Mahmoud Darwish. Which form speaks to you and the material you have in mind? With whom do you find yourself having a mental dialogue? Could you 'answer back' in form? Arguably, when you start writing long, especially as the long poem is such an open form in English, you should have no sense of outcome, but should allow the material to take you where it needs to. However, I think a model, or destination, is useful at first. After a while, you'll get a sense of what the poetic unit is like; of where you are in a piece and of what that piece, as well as the material it engages, needs. The predictable questions of pace, diction, variety and flexibility are at first only part of the process for redrafting. But gradually they will become internalized, just as the demands of sonnet form, say, do. Just like any other form, the long poem, whether narrative or not, justifies itself in the end by its own poetic necessity.

20 Into print

Publish and be damned.

The Duke of Wellington, 1825,
responding to blackmail threats

No poet starts with a book. That's because poems aren't usually book-length, but poem-length. This being so, why not publish them as you finish them? The only reasons not to are that you don't want an audience, or you (or somebody else) feel they aren't good enough. If the former, you wouldn't want to publish a book either. If the latter: well, if they're *really* not good enough for magazine publication they certainly aren't ready to be published as a book.

Unless, that is, you pay to be published in book form. This is called vanity publishing and, as well as presenting many traps to the unwary (vanity publishers are known to the book trade and their books aren't available in bookshops or on Amazon, nor are they reviewed), it simply doesn't count as publishing. Think of it this way: if you go and buy yourself a silver cup from the jewellers – you haven't actually *won* anything at all. You want the *endorsement* of seeing your work in print, so that you know you really can call yourself a writer. That's a hard-won prize: a real achievement. If you 'buy the cup' by paying to be published, no one has awarded it to you. In literary publishing, someone else, somebody who knows about poetry, decides you're good enough to be in a magazine or to have a book published. In academia, this

209

is called 'peer-review': scholarship has to be of a high professional standard if it's to be taken seriously. Professionals, with knowledge of the subject, check it out. It is *this* accolade you want as a poet.

Or do you just want the object, the beautiful book? In which case, go direct to a printer's. It's lots cheaper than paying a vanity publisher to act as middleman, and you get to choose how the book will look. You don't pretend that you're being published, either. That matters: because false consciousness is the enemy of good writing, and it will seep into the next poems you write. At some level, if you pay to have a book printed, you'll know there's some pretence going on. You'll feel your writing wasn't good enough for the real thing. You'll undermine yourself by the very thing that you believed could give you confidence, and your poems won't have the ring of conviction.

But there are a couple of caveats to this. The first is that this advice is specific to the economic West. In countries with little state subsidy of the arts and low per capita incomes, such as Nigeria or Romania, different norms apply. Here you may have to pay the publisher who *accepts* your book – even though gaining that acceptance is difficult and prestigious – because they can't afford printing costs. Second, wherever you live, *collective* self-publishing – when a group, particularly of younger writers with a mission, meets up and decides to publish together – does not count as 'vanity' and can be highly creative. The difference is to be found in two areas. One is the introduction of *literary judgement*. If, for example, your writing group decides to publish an anthology in aid of a local appeal, or if you and other writers you admire from student days stay in touch and decide to found a magazine, you'll find yourself, from the outset, making decisions about which writing you think is the best. Second, a result of group work, and indeed of any literary decision-making, is that you always have *a public* in mind, whether they're the readers who'll buy your themed anthology or young radicals you'd like to attract to your new house style. As members of writing workshops know, the mere fact of making your own writing public is a radical step towards *making it real*. Writing groups' anthologies don't get as widely read or reviewed as anthologies, and in particular collections, from mainstream publishers. But they are *respectable*. You can add them to your writer's biography – and in this way they will help you be published elsewhere. They can make a splash, too, when they're properly launched – especially if you have contacts, such as tutors, who are well known in poetry circles and can alert at least some of the people they know.

'Little magazines' are more interesting still. The Poetry Library in London has lists, and in many case examples, of most of the country's poetry magazines. There's also a historical collection of journals at the British Library. Much of the most creative work in poetry has been hot-housed by various periodicals. In the days of Modernism, T.S. Eliot edited *The Criterion*; Stephen Spender edited the very international *Encounter*; Ian Hamilton founded and edited *The Review*, and its successor *The New Review*, and discovered many of the senior names in British poetry today. When Alan Ross edited *London Magazine*, his discoveries included Sylvia Plath. Each had a house style, which they promulgated forcefully. There *are* limits to what such magazines can do – the mere term 'little' suggests something inward-looking and self-restricting, after all – since it's obviously not the case that there's only one kind of writing that is any good. A quick glance at any school history of English Literature proves great poetry has been written in a variety of forms and according to very varied poetics. To say nothing of the rest of the world. But these magazines can open doors for both readers and writers.

It's important to know which suit your own writing (easy: the ones that are full of poetry you respond to) and *also* which are the current powerhouses, even for kinds of writing you don't write or particularly enjoy yourself. Use a library like the Poetry Library – the shelves of the specialist bookshops can be excellent, but are limited by commercial factors – to browse your way towards a mental map of little magazines.

Subscribe to as many as you can afford (two? three?), perhaps making different choices each year. Subscriptions are not expensive when you compare them to the price of a single writing workshop; and, if you subscribe to at least one of the major magazines, you'll be reading poetry that should raise the stakes for you, inspire you and introduce you to new possibilities and poets – as well as allowing you to decide which books you'd like to buy without making expensive errors.

If you've an appetite for founding a little magazine of your own, all this reading will give you a feel for the kind of journal you'd like to produce, and whether something similar already exists. Editing a little magazine can be very rewarding, but may also be costly in time and money. It's a good idea to find collaborators to share the strain – and the creative thinking. If you're going to edit another magazine of British poetry, be clear what your pitch will be. Are you iconoclasts, and if so what do you believe in? Or do you have a specific geographical or other remit, such as poetry from Tyneside or by Welsh women? Many of the great editors take over existing magazines; but two little magazines that have been success stories in recent years are *Thumbscrew* – led by critical practice, published by smart young men out of Oxford, it challenged the consensus of the 1990s – and *The Wolf*, which does the opposite. Led by poetry practice, it doesn't back away from the metropolitan centre of the profession, but makes the mixture anew, with greater internationalism, a young editor's perspective, and more porous borders than the very established magazines. It's easier for an unknown to be published there alongside very distinguished verse. But these are just two models – your own would have to be different again in order to succeed.

Anyone who's ever worked on a poetry magazine, even if only volunteering over a summer, will support the standard procedures for submitting poems. Once you've worked on a journal, you understand why they exist and how sensible they are. *So here we go.* Submit six poems, typed, on one side of A4, with your name and address (or email) on *each* sheet. Put the best poem on top. Number the pages of long poems. Write a brief covering letter in which you a) get the name of the editor right, thus indicating you have bothered sufficiently about a magazine that you'd like to bother with you to at least glance at it or its website; b) supply a short sentence or paragraph of writer biography; and c) do not add anything tricky or aggressive. Send it all off with an s.a.e. large enough for the magazine to squeeze your returned typescripts into (the best size is A5). It must be an s.a.e.: not stamps and an address sticker, nor an old envelope they need to find sellotape for. Don't just give an email address, or airily permit the editors to recycle your poems. That's all extra work: and recycling can be *your* responsibility, if you genuinely care about it, as indeed you should. Do not submit by email, except to e-zines, unless the magazine makes *clear* that this is acceptable. Above all, do not submit in some unconventional way that the magazine does not ask for, and then complain if your submission gets lost.

Magazines are run by dedicated, over-worked individuals who have some sort of belief in poetry beyond the naked careerism of 'my own poems and nothing but'. Some periodicals are Arts Council funded: but, like all charities and voluntary agencies, they have little spare money. You would be horrified at the working conditions if you stepped into the offices of even the most famous among them. So, do not ask them to supply the stationery that you're too mean to supply. Do not be rude to them: they work harder than you can imagine. Do not try stunts to make your poems stand out. Any worthwhile magazine will practise integrity in dealing with submissions. It's in their interests to publish the best stuff because that is what makes them better magazines. Do not ask for an individual tutorial feedback. Though *Poetry Review* is far ahead of the field in the 60,000 unsolicited submissions it receives annually, most serious magazines receive in the high hundreds or thousands. It would be impossible to read everything properly if one also had to write a fully detailed – and kindly worded – essay on each. Also, respect your own

213

professionalism. You shouldn't be asking for free lessons from an editor. If you feel you're at that stage – and there's nothing wrong with that feeling – find a tutor!

It's all too easy to feel, after the repeated rejections that are always part of this process, that editors are powerful and to be resented. It's important to turn this feeling inside out whenever you notice it. Bitterness will curdle your writing, and can produce the kind of defensiveness that makes you disengage from the wider national scene and settle for whatever pleases your local writing group, for example. It's also inaccurate. Most editors worked extremely hard to achieve that role, either by founding and building up a magazine or by developing a whole range of skills (things like reviewing, writing and related editing or publishing work) over years of professional practice in order to be skilled enough for the job. Unless you're prepared to follow – or find and develop – such routes yourself, it's disingenuous to harbour resentment. After all, magazine editors spend their working lives enabling *other people's* poetry – and not because they can't do it themselves. From Eliot to Raine, most of the great editors have been poets themselves.

But which magazines to send to? *The Writer's Handbook*, published annually, has good advice and reasonably comprehensive listings, but nothing beats the simple test of interleaving your own poem among the pages of a magazine to see whether it belongs there. The classic advice is that you don't send the same poems to more than one magazine at a time – 'no multiple submissions' – but since magazines can have a long decision cycle, and editors rarely pick the same poem, some small overlap is permissible – providing you let the other magazine know *instantly* if a poem submitted in this way is accepted. An even more useful piece of advice is to turn the poems round. As soon as a rejection comes in, send them back out again somewhere else. That way, everything is always in process and full of possibility.

Finally, start small. It's unlikely your very first poems will make the biggest magazines, but there are many that specialize in emerging writers. This is a difficult thing to conceptualize: when you've produced your best poem to date, it's hard to believe that you need to set a limit on where it's likely to end up. But – harder still to believe – you *will* produce even better poems further down the line. Poetry is a constant, and continuing, apprenticeship, and we improve through periodic step-changes that are necessarily unexpected – since if you knew you could do *that*, you'd be doing it already. Your future development is bound to occur in the most surprising ways. You may turn out to be a completely other poet than the kind you thought you were.

But that's in the future. Right now, you're the poet you are, with a dozen or more acceptances from magazines or placings in poetry competitions. The latter *are* invidious – but worth going in for if you know the judge's work and it's the kind of thing you like and admire. That makes it likely they'll respond to your kind of work, too. Again, it's probably better not to enter the big three – the National, the Arvon and the Bridport – until you've had successes in smaller competitions, such as those run by the larger magazines. After all, every entry costs you money! There's little point either in trying to subvert these competitions. Even if your very best poem is a haiku, there's no point in entering it for a competition for poems of standard length (generally, up to forty lines). It simply won't win against a poem of equal merit but that does the work of thirty-eight lines. Riddles, pastiches and rants against what you might perceive to be the poetry consensus won't win either. There's nothing original about resentment.

Once you have around a dozen publications and competition placements under your belt, your poetry may be moving towards a manuscript both in terms of *quantity* of finished, worked poems and in terms of their track record of *quality*. Your next step is to turn this pile of poems into a book. Emerging poets often ask, 'Why should I do this? Can't an editor spot talent from the poems themselves?' Editors *can* spot talent; and usually *do* work on manuscripts they accept

– though some do much more than others. But *talent* isn't what makes you a poet. *Accomplishment* is. You need to demonstrate that you can make a book – and the only way to do that is by doing so: in manuscript. Because you're an unknown at this stage, a pile of poems will tell an editor nothing – except that you didn't have the pride, self-respect or enthusiasm to turn them into a manuscript. Even if your individual poems are stunning, this will send out a warning sign. *Why* would you want to avoid this interesting, creative work? What does it suggest about your commitment to the idea of a book, let alone the whole project of poetry? How does the editor know, unless you demonstrate it via a manuscript, that you have the personal resources to work (with him) on turning these poems into a collection? Besides all this, a pile of poems, not ordered and formatted to appear at their best, will find it hard to compete, even in terms of displaying talent, with the properly formatted submissions that do come in.

So let's start with the basics. Length is the most important. You need about sixty to sixty-five pages of poems: printing comes cheapest in multiples of sixteen pages, but most serious publishers will carry a page or more blank at the end of a book. You also need to allow (in a notional eighty pages) for title page, acknowledgements, contents. Count for a half-title page, dedication and their versos too, but don't include these materials in the manuscript – unless you have an epigraph for the book as a whole, in which case *do* include that on a separate page – as to do so looks pretentious. You don't need Oscar-style acknowledgements to your nearest and dearest at this stage, either. Just the CV of your book: where poems have been published or awarded. This matters, as it's your own track record, too. Check in the books on your shelves for suitably understated wording. Good, workmanlike formulas include: 'Acknowledgements are due to the editors of the following publications. . .' 'Some of these poems first appeared in the following publications . . .'

Especially if you write long poems, or poems long enough

to reach the bottom of an A4 page, change your text box to accommodate roughly the number of lines of poetry a *book* will have (around forty, on a page without a title). This usually means raising the bottom margin of the text box. Also, if you write exceptionally long lines, check the number of characters a usual page permits across a line (you need only count this once, but use poetry books from more than one publisher) and move your right-hand margin in accordingly. Sort out your line run-ons (right-justified) so that they don't look like new lines. *Now* you're counting more accurately.

Now you know the space you have to work with. Print out all your likely poems. Find a huge space – probably a floor, if you have one that is child- and animal-free – and lay them all out (I stack subsequent pages under first pages of long poems when I'm doing this). Which are the strongest? Pick out your favourites and also the ones that have done well for you. Now think of the opening of the book that will introduce you. Which is your best opening poem? It probably won't be long, but it will be clear as a bell, and will set the tone – and probably the topic – of the book. Now, what follows it best (never mind keeping your powder dry for later on . . .)? Which poem makes it look best and looks best next to it? Now you have two poems: the start of a sequence. Can you hear 'your' voice speaking through them, number one to number two? What keeps this level up? And now a fourth? Now go back and skim-read through again. Still feeling good? Then – on to the fifth. If you begin to feel this running order is too slick, too easy or too thematically one-note, have a look through your material for a poem that would counteract this tendency. Try it in place – does it work?

This is how the running order of collections, anthologies and magazines is built up. It's a step-by-step set of practical creative decisions about what works. As the sequence goes on, of course, it gets harder. More of the good stuff has been used up; there's less room for manoeuvre. All of a sudden you reach a point where you can't go any further. The remaining poems would embarrass you if they were in print. Or there may be just a couple you can't seem to fit together at the point in the running order you've got to. If they're strong poems you don't want to lose, try each at various earlier points in the sequence. At this point, they may create such knock-on problems of ordering (that funny poem can't go after that elegy, etc.) that the whole run seems to collapse. Don't panic. Leave the manuscript in this provisional order and come back to it fresh the next day.

Ordering is surprisingly demanding because it requires you to keep *all* the poems involved in your head, so as to feel what might belong where. This keeping everything in mind will probably show you that your collection has certain characteristic themes. Think about the manuscript's character, both poetical and topical, as you order it. What would strengthen this unitary identity? Is there anything missing that you still need to write? Writing *for a book* is not at all unusual. For example: you may find that the register of the manuscript as a whole is too measured. Not enough of your passion has come through. Or it feels insubstantial – and you need to supply some ballast. Or maybe a particular success for you is the new set of villanelles you've been writing: just one more and they'd feel like something linking the manuscript, rather than a coincidental cluster.

This way of thinking about the whole book allows you to come up with titles, too. You may have one already. If not, look for something that will characterize the book, and raise the stakes for it, by being memorable and clear in its own terms. For help with this, look at existing book titles. Which sound so provocative you want to open the book immediately? Which are forgettable? Try out the titles of the individual poems. Is one of them distinctive enough, and the poem it titles strong enough, to take on the highly visible role of title poem? This is traditionally the key to a collection. Some poets simply name a book after the strongest poem in it. But what happens if the main theme of your manuscript is explored through a number of smaller poems? You might be able to use a phrase or line from within a poem instead. Better to find your title *somewhere* within the manuscript than to bring it from outside, though you can always 'cheat' and retrospectively change the title of a poem if you think up an ideal name for the book later. It doesn't matter if the new 'title poem' was already published in its old form: poets often publish early versions of poems.

Now – where are you going to send your book? Look at the biographical notes of poets who publish in the same magazines as yourself. Look at the publishers' lists. This time you can't multiple-submit, so it will pay you to pick the publisher most likely to take you on. Above all, be realistic. When all your creative work is done, number the pages, print out the manuscript on single-sided A4, and use a spine-binder of some kind to put it together. Your cover letter won't be very different from the one you send to magazines – though it does no harm, and indeed helps you clarify your own thinking, to add a sentence about why you'd like to be part of *this* list in particular. Enclose a large s.a.e. for manuscript return, just as in a magazine submission (only larger, of course, and with the correct postage). Now sit back and wait. You may have to wait a long time – six months' minimum – because any manuscript that is good enough to be considered seriously will go through a series of consultations and readings before acceptance.

The publishers won't keep you posted during this wait because so many false hopes would be raised, and because picking a book by a new poet is a gradual process. So don't pester them in the meantime. You are not an exception. The more time they have to spend telling you that no, there's no decision yet, the less they have for the actual work of editing. And the more difficult you are to deal with, the less likely they are to see you as a good risk. Every publisher gambles their business – or charity – with every book they publish. That book may compromise their reputation for quality; it may also be an albatross that doesn't sell, and limits the other work they can do. So they need to know that they are investing in a book – and also a poet – to stay the course. They need to know you are going to develop and go further. They also need to know that you're going to be reasonably

OK to deal with, for everyone from festival promoters to local newspapers, so that they can rely on you to go out into the poetry world and make your work visible. This is not about being a young beauty and a great charmer. But it *is* about professionalism and courtesy. In a field in which there will always be many other writers eager to take your place, every poet needs to be good to do business with. In the end it's this, along with the hard graft of writing as well as you possibly can, that will allow you to build up the undeniable body of work that makes a poet.

A third way to establish your track record – after magazine publication and competitions – is through readings. Having had a book published makes this much easier. But if you live in a city, it shouldn't be too hard anyway. Find your local open mic and reading nights. Read *every time,* so that you get better and better. If there's a launch for a magazine you're in, go along and, when there's an open slot, read your poem from the magazine, even if you aren't one of the better-known contributors invited to start the evening. If there's no reading venue or group in your local town, think about setting one up, maybe inviting a well-known poet once a month, adding an open mic session in the second half. Talk to your local arts centre or library or college; see if there's grant funding of any kind. Become known as someone who's *really involved* in poetry – and people will start to come to you with ideas for collaboration, and with opportunities.

This all takes a lot of energy. Emerging and working as a poet can be a tough, discouraging process. It's important to ignore stories of overnight success. They rarely are: just because the literary editor of a broadsheet hasn't heard of a poet doesn't mean their tutors, and peers and readers in the magazine, reading and competition worlds haven't. It's also important to ignore crass nepotism where it occurs (and it does) if you don't want to go mad. In the end, no matter the shortcuts anyone else takes, *if you have the body of work, you have become a poet.* Good luck!

Appendix: listings

First and indispensably, you need an up-to-date edition of *The Writer's Handbook*, published by Macmillan, and internet access. With a combination of these, you can create your own ramifying and evolving database. These are just some starting points.

1 Publishers

All these publishers have substantial lists of poetry. However, their reputations and house styles vary tremendously. They also have differing reading policies for submissions. Never send work to a publisher until you've checked *both* the kinds of poetry they publish, *and* their up-to-date submission guidelines (which should be available on their websites).

Anvil Press Poetry
Neptune House, 70 Royal Hill, London SE10 8RF
Tel: 020 8469 3033
Website: www.anvilpresspoetry.com/
Email: info@anvilpresspoetry.com
Editor: Peter Jay

Arc Publications
Nanholme Mill, Shaw Wood Road, Todmorden, Lancashire OL14 6DA
Tel: 01706 812338
Website: www.arcpublications.co.uk

Email: info@arcpublications.co.uk
Editor: Tony Ward

Bloodaxe Books
Highgreen, Tarset, Northumberland NE48 1RP
Tel: 01434 240500
Website: www.bloodaxebooks.com
Email: editor@bloodaxebooks.com
Editor: Neil Astley

Canongate Books
14 High Street, Edinburgh EH1 1TE
Tel: 0131 557 5111
Website: www.canongate.net
Email: info@canongate.co.uk
Editor: Jamie Byng

Carcanet Press
4th Floor, Alliance House, 30 Cross Street,
Manchester M2 7AP
Tel: 0161 834 8730
Website: www.carcanet.co.uk
Email: info@carcanet.co.uk
Editor: Michael Schmidt

Chatto & Windus
Random House, 20 Vauxhall Bridge Road, London SW1V 2SA
Tel: 020 7840 8400
Website: www.randomhouse.co.uk/poetry/home.htm
Email: enquiries@randomhouse.co.uk

Enitharmon Press
26b Caversham Road, London NW5 2DU
Tel: 020 7482 5967
Website: www.enitharmon.co.uk
Email: books@enitharmon.co.uk
Editor: Stephen Stuart-Smith

Faber & Faber
Bloomsbury House, 74–77 Great Russell Street,
London WC1B 3DA
Tel: 020 7927 3800
Website: www.faber.co.uk
Email: contact@faber.co.uk
Editor: Paul Keegan

Jonathan Cape
Random House, 20 Vauxhall Bridge Road, London SW1V 2SA
Tel: 020 7840 8400
Website:www.randomhouse.co.uk/poetry/home.htm
Email: enquiries@randomhouse.co.uk
Editor: Robin Robertson

Macmillan
The Macmillan Building, 4 Crinan Street, London N1 9XW
Tel: 020 7843 3600
Website: www.macmillan.com

Penguin Books Ltd
80 The Strand, London WC2R 0RL
Website: www.penguin.co.uk

Picador
Pan Macmillan Ltd, 20 New Wharf Road, London N1 9RR
Tel: 020 7014 6000
Website:www.panmacmillan.com/imprints/#PICADOR
Poetry Editor: Don Paterson

Salt Publishing
PO Box 937, Great Wilbraham PDO, Cambridge CB1 5JX
Tel: 01223 882220
Website: www.saltpublishing.com
Email: jen@saltpublishing.com
Editor: Chris Hamilton-Emery

Shearsman Books
58 Velwell Road, Exeter EX4 4LD
Tel: 01392 434511
Website: www.shearsman.com
Email: editor@shearsman.com
Editor: Tony Frazer

Shoestring Press
19 Devonshire Avenue, Beeston, Nottingham NG9 1BS
Tel: 01159 251827
Website: www.shoestring-press.co.uk
Email: info@shoestringpress.co.uk

Stride Publications
4b Tremayne Close, Devoran, Truro, Cornwall TR3 6QE
Website: www.stridebooks.co.uk
Email: editor@stridebooks.co.uk
Editor: Rupert Loydell

2 Magazines

These magazines are a tiny fraction of the little magazine
scene. For details of others, see the Poetry Library's listings,
either on-line or on-site in London. However, though the
publications listed here vary tremendously in reputation,
standard and style, they are by and large the ones that editors
will have heard of, ones that attract a decent readership and
that are therefore worth approaching. Editorial names and
addresses in the magazine world are more volatile than those
in book publishing, so make sure you have up-to-date details
before submitting. Additionally, magazines have much more
pronounced remits for geographical areas and styles of writ-
ing than book lists. It is essential that you check these out
before submitting. This list, for example, includes magazines
especially for women, gay or BME writers, Postmodernists,
Welsh and Scottish writers.

Acumen
6 The Mount, Higher Furzeham, Brixham, South Devon
TQ5 8QY
4 Thornhill Bridge Wharf, London N1 0RU
Website: www.acumen-poetry.co.uk
Editors: Patricia and William Oxley

Agenda
The Wheelwrights, Fletching Street, Mayfield, East Sussex
TN20 6TL
Tel: 01435 873703
Website: www.agendapoetry.co.uk
Email: editor@agendapoetry.co.uk
Editor: Patricia McCarthy

Ambit
17 Priory Gardens, Highgate, London N6 5QY
Website: www.ambitmagazine.co.uk
Email: info@ambitmagazine.co.uk
Editors: Martin Bax and Kate Pemberton

Angel Exhaust
21 Querneby Road, Nottingham NG3 5JA
Email: aduncan@pinko.org
Editor: Andrew Duncan

Arete
8 New College Lane, Oxford OX1 3BN
Tel: 01865 289193
Fax: 01865 289194
Website: www.aretemagazine.com
Email: craig.raine@new.ox.ac.uk
Editor: Craig Raine

Banipal: Magazine of Modern Arab Literature
PO Box 22300, London W13 8ZQ
Tel: 020 8568 9747

Fax: +44 (0)20 8567 8509
Website: www.banipal.co.uk
Email editor@banipal.co.uk
Editor: Margaret Obank

Brittle Star
PO Box 56108, London E17 0AY
Website: www.brittlestar.org.uk
Email: magazine@brittlestar.org.uk
Editors: Jacqueline Gabbitas, Louisa Hooper, Tina Tse, David Floyd, Martin Parker

Calabash: For Writers of African and Asian Descent
Centreprise, 136–8 Kingsland High Street, London E8 2NS
Tel: 0207 249 6572
Email: literature@centreprisetrust.org.uk
Editor: Sharon Duggal

Chapman
4 Broughton Place, Edinburgh EH1 3RX
Tel: 0131 557 2207
Fax: 0131 556965
Website: www.chapman-pub.co.uk
Email: chapman-pub@blueyonder.co.uk
Editor: Joy Hendry

Chroma: queer writing
PO Box 44655, London N16 0WQ
Tel: 020 7193 7642
Website: www.chromajournal.co.uk
Email: editor@chromajournal.co.uk
Editor: Shaun Levin

Cyphers
3 Selskar Terrace, Ranelagh, Dublin 6, Ireland
Editors: Leland Bardwell, Eilean Ni Chuilleanain, Pearse Hutchinson, McDara Woods

Edinburgh Review
22 Buccleuch Place, Edinburgh EH8 9LN
Tel: 0131 651 1415
Website: www.edinburghreview.org.uk
Email: edinburgh.review@ed.ac.uk
Editor: Ronald Turnbull
Assistant Editor: Karina Dent

Envoi
Ty Meirion, Glan Yr Afon, Tanygrisiau, Blaenau Ffestiniog
LL41 3SU
Website: www.envoipoetry.com
Editor: Jan Fortune-Wood

Exiled Ink! For exiled writers
31 Hallswelle Road, London NW11 0DH
Website: www.exiledwriters.co.uk
Email: Jennifer@exiledwriters.fsnet.co.uk
Editor: Jennifer Langer

The Haiku Quarterly
39 Exmouth Street, Swindon, Wiltshire SN1 3PU
Editor: Kevin Bailey

The Interpreter's House
19 The Paddox, Squitchey Lane, Oxford OX2 7PN
Website: www.interpretershouse.org.uk
Editor: Merryn Williams

Iota
1 Lodge Farm, Snitterfield, Stratford-on-Avon, Warwickshire
CV37 0LR
Website: www.iotapoetry.co.uk
Email: iotapoetry@aol.com
Editors: Bob Mee and Jane Murch

Irish Pages
The Linen Hall Library, 17 Donegal Square North, Belfast
BT1 5GB
Website: www.irishpages.org
Editor: Chris Agee

London Magazine
70 Wargrave Rd, London N15 6UB
Email: admin@thelondonmagazine.net

London Review of Books
28 Little Russell Street, London WC1A 2HN
Website: www.lrb.co.uk
Email: edit@lrb.co.uk
Editor: Mary-Kay Wilmers

Magma
43 Keslake Rd, London NW6 6DH
Website: www.magmapoetry.com
Email: magmapoetry@ntlworld.com
Electronic submissions: contributions@magmapoetry.com
Editor: David Boll and guest editors

Metre
Dept of English, University of Hull, Hull HU6 7RX
Editors: David Wheatley and Justin Quinn

Modern Poetry in Translation
Queen's College, Oxford OX1 4AW
Website: www.mptmagazine.com
Editors: David and Helen Constantine

Mslexia: for women who write
PO Box 656, Newcastle upon Tyne NE99 1PZ
Tel: 0191 261 6656
Fax: 0191 261 6636
Website: www.mslexia.co.uk

Email: postbag@mslexia.demon.co.uk

New Welsh Review
PO Box 170, Aberystwyth, Ceredigion SY23 1WZ
Tel: 01970 628410
Website: www.newelshreview.com
Email: editor@newwelshreview.com
Editor: Kathryn Gray

The North
The Poetry Business, The Studio, Byram Arcade, Westgate,
Huddersfield HD1 1ND
Tel: 01484 434840
Fax: 01484 426566
Website: www.poetrybusiness.co.uk
Email: edit@poetrybusiness.co.uk
Editors: Peter Sansom and Janet Fisher

Orbis
17 Greenhow Avenue, West Kirby, Wirral CH48 5EL
Email: carolebaldock@hotmail.com
Editor: Carole Baldock

P.N. Review
Department of English, University of Glasgow, 5 University
Gardens, Glasgow G12 8QH
Website: www.pnreview.co.uk
Editor: Michael Schmidt

Planet: The Welsh Internationalist
PO Box 44, Aberystwyth, Ceredigion, Dyfed SY23 3ZZ
Tel: 01970 611255
Website: www.planetmagazine.org.uk
Email: planet.enquiries@planetmagazine.org.uk

Poetry Express: Quarterly from Survivors' Poetry
Survivors' Poetry, Studio 11, Bickerton House

25–27 Bickerton Road, Archway, London N19 5JT
Tel: 020 7281 4654
Website: www.survivorspoetry.com
Email: info@survivorspoetry.org.uk
Editors: Alan Morrison and Roy Holland

Poetry London
6 Daniels Road, London SE15 3LR
Website: www.poetrylondon.co.uk
Email: editors@poetrylondon.co.uk

Poetry Nottingham
11 Orkney Close, Stenson Fields, Derby DE24 3LW
Editor: Adrian Buckner

Poetry Review
The Poetry Society, 22 Betterton Street, London WC2H 9BX
Website: www.poetrysoc.com
Email: poetryreview@poetrysoc.com
Editor: Fiona Sampson

Poetry Salzburg Review
99 Mitre Road, London SE1 8PT
Website: www.poetrysalzburg.com/psr
Email: katermurr_uk@yahoo.co.uk
Editor: David Miller

Poetry Scotland
91–3 Main St, Callander FK17 8BQ
Website: www.poetryscotland.co.uk
Editor: Sally Evans

Poetry Wales
11 Park Avenue, Porthcawl CF36 3EP
Website: www.poetrywales.co.uk
Email: poetrywales@seren-books.com
Editor: Zoe Skoulding

Rialto
PO Box 309, Aylesham, Norwich NR11 6LN
Website: www.therialto.co.uk
Editor: Michael Mackmin

Scintilla
Little Wentwood Farm, Llantrisant, Usk, Monmouthshire NP15 1ND
Website: www.cf.ac.uk./encap/scintilla
Email: anne.cluysenaar@virgin.net
Editor: Anne Cluysenaar

Second Light: for older women writers
9 Greendale Close, London SE22 8TG
Email: dilyswood@tiscali.co.uk
Editor: Dilys Wood

Shearsman
58 Velwell Road, Exeter EX4 4LD
Website: www.shearsman.com
Editor: Tony Frazer

The SHOP
Skeagh, Schull, County Cork, Ireland
Website: www.theshop-poetry-magazine.ie
Editors: John and Hilary Wakeman

Smiths Knoll
Goldings, Goldings Lane, Leiston, Suffolk IP16 4EB
Editors: Michael Laskey and Joanna Cutts

Stand
School of English, University of Leeds, Leeds LS2 9JT
Tel: 0113 233 4794
Fax: 0113 233 4791
Email: stand@leeds.ac.uk
Editor: Jon Glover

Staple
114–116 St Stephen's Road, Sneinton, Nottingham NG2 4JS
Website: www.staplemagazine.wordpress.com
Editor: Wayne Burrows

The Stinging Fly
PO Box 6016, Dublin 8, Ireland
Website: www.stingingfly.org
Email: stingingfly@hotmail.com
Editor: Declan Meade

Tears in the Fence
38 Hod View, Stourpaine, Blandford Forum, Dorset DT11 8TN
Editor: David Caddy

Temenos Academy Review: for metaphysical poetry
The Temenos Academy, PO Box 203, Ashford, Kent TN25 5ZT
Tel: 01233 813663
Email: stephenovery@onetel.com

The Times Literary Supplement
Times House, Pennington Square, London E98 1BS

Wasafiri
The Open University in London, 1–11 Hawley Crescent,
Camden Town, London NW1 8NP
Tel: 020 7556 6110
Website: www.wasafiri.org
Email: www.wasafiri@open.ac.uk
Editor: Susheila Nasata

The Wolf
3 Holly Mansions, Fortune Green Road, West Hampstead,
London NW6 1UB
Website: www.wolfmagazine.co.uk
Email: editor@wolfmagazine.co.uk
Editor: James Byrne

Writing in Education
NAWE, PO Box 1, Sheriff Hutton, York YO60 7YU
Tel: 01653 618429
Website: www.nawe.co.uk
Editors: Liz Cashdan, Kathy Flann, Katherine Gallagher,
Bryan Podmore, Sarah Salway. Reviews: Debjani Chatterjee

Young Writer: Magazine for young people
Glebe House, Church Road, Weobley, Hereford HR4 8SD
Tel/Fax: 01544 318901
Website: www.youngwriter.org
Email: editor@youngwriter.org

3 Useful organizations

The Poetry Society of Great Britain
22 Betterton Street, London WC2H 9BX
Tel: 020 7420 9895
Website: www.poetrysociety.org.uk
Email: info@poetrysociety.org.uk

Yr Academi Gymreig/The Welsh Academy
3rd Floor, Mount Stuart House, Mount Stuart Square, Cardiff
CF10 5FQ
Tel: 029 2047 2266
Website: www.academi.org

The Scottish Poetry Library
Crichton's Close, Canongate, Edinburgh EH8 8DT
Tel: 0131 557 2876
Website: www.spl.org.uk
Email: reception@spl.org.uk

The Poetry Library
Level 5, Royal Festival Hall, London SE1 8XX
Tel: 020 7921 0943

Website: www.poetrylibrary.org.uk

National Association of Writers in Education
NAWE, PO Box 1, Sheriff Hutton, York YO60 7YU
Tel: 01653 618429
Website: www.nawe.co.uk

The Arvon Foundation
42a Buckingham Palace Road, London SW1W 0RE
Tel: 020 7931 7611
Website: www.arvonfoundation.org
Email: london@arvonfoundation.org

Ty Newydd Writers' Centre
Llanystumdwy, Criccieth, Gwynedd LL52 0LW
Tel: 01766 522811
Website: www.tynewydd.org/english
Email: post@tynewydd.org

For MA courses, see *The Writers' and Artists' Yearbook.*

Index